Beholding Beauty

Beholding Beauty

Worshiping God through the Arts

JASON R. McCONNELL

WIPF & STOCK · Eugene, Oregon

BEHOLDING BEAUTY
Worshiping God through the Arts

Copyright © 2022 Wipf and Stock Publishers. All rights reserved. Except for brief quotations in critical publications or reviews, no part of this book may be reproduced in any manner without prior written permission from the publisher. Write: Permissions, Wipf and Stock Publishers, 199 W. 8th Ave., Suite 3, Eugene, OR 97401.

Wipf & Stock
An Imprint of Wipf and Stock Publishers
199 W. 8th Ave., Suite 3
Eugene, OR 97401

www.wipfandstock.com

PAPERBACK ISBN: 978-1-6667-3064-7
HARDCOVER ISBN: 978-1-6667-2240-6
EBOOK ISBN: 978-1-6667-2242-0

02/25/22

Images:
"On a Hill Far Away" by Cornie McCarley. Used by permission.
"Concert in the Gorge" by Bill Higginson and Olga Rybalko. Used by permission.
"Longing for the Feast" by Jocelyn Yagel. Used by permission.

Unless otherwise indicated, Scripture quotations are from the Holy Bible, New International Version, NIV. Copyright 1973, 1984, 2011 by Biblica, Inc. Used by permission of Zondervan and Biblica. All rights reserved worldwide. www.zondervan.com; Biblica.com. Italics in the NIV text have been added by the author for emphasis.

Scripture quotations labeled The Message are from THE MESSAGE copyright 1993, 2002, 2018 by Eugene Peterson. Used by permission of NavPress, represented by Tyndale House Publishers. All rights reserved.

To
Dr. David Horn,
the designer and director of
the Ockenga Fellows Program
at Gordon-Conwell Theological Seminary.

Your creativity and imagination has inspired all of us
to behold beauty as we bear witness to the gospel of Jesus Christ.

Contents

List of Illustrations		ix
List of Contributors		xi
Preface		xiii
Acknowledgments		xvii
Introduction: A Brief Reflection on Beauty and Longing		xix
	DAVID HORN	
Chapter 1	God: The Original Artist	1
	JASON MCCONNELL	
Chapter 2	Colorful Silence: The Art of Painting	14
	DEVON MCCARLEY	
Chapter 3	The Divine Sculptor: The Art of Sculpture	24
	JOSHUA CAHAN	
Chapter 4	Adequately Clothed: The Art of Fashion	35
	MONICA ROBERTS	
Chapter 5	The Dance of Redemption: The Art of Ballet	47
	JONATHAN ROMIG	
Chapter 6	Losing Sight of the Choreographer: The Art of Choreography	59
	TRIP WEILER	
Chapter 7	How Long, O Lord: The Art of Poetry	69
	MANNY DAPHNIS	
Chapter 8	The Power of a Song: The Art of Songwriting	79
	TYLER SMITH	

Chapter 9	To See What You See: The Art of Popular Music Timothy Bogertman	91
Chapter 10	The Story of God in One Meal: The Art of the Novel Richard J. Harrington	103
Chapter 11	Stories that Unveil: The Art of the Short Story David Coons	114
Chapter 12	Drama Is Required: The Art of Theater Jeff Miller	123
Chapter 13	Mercy and Truth Have Met Together: The Art of Cinema Timothy D. Bresnahan	133
Chapter 14	The Invitation of the Table-Setting God: Culinary Art Sean Roberts	144
Chapter 15	The Great Vintner: The Art of Winemaking Brian Bethke	160
Chapter 16	The Aroma of Aesthetic Extravagance: The Art of Fragrance Jason McConnell	171
Chapter 17	Reclaiming the Arts Through Worship Kenneth J. Barnes	182
Bibliography		189

List of Illustrations

Lauterbrunnen by Alexandre Calame	xix
Creation of the Animals by Il Tintoretto	1
On a Hill Far Away by Cornie D. McCarley	14
Hand of God by François Auguste René Rodin	24
God's Curse, Adam And Eve by James Tisso	35
Four Dancers by Edgar Degas	47
El Jaleo by John Singer Sargent	59
King David in Prayer by Pieter de Grebber	69
King David Playing the Harp by Peter Paul Rubens and Jan Boekhorst	79
Concert at the Gorge by Bill Higginson and Olga Rybalko	91
Crime and Punishment by Nikolay Karazin	103
The Parable of the Sower by Pieter Brugal the Elder	114
Photograph of the Bishop and Jean Valjean in the musical *Les Misérables*	123
Collage of still photographs from Gabriel Axel's *Babette's Feast*	133
Longing for the Feast by Jocelin Yagel	144
The Wedding Feast at Cana by Julius Schnorr von Carolsfeld	160
Christ in the House of Simon by Deiric Bouts the Elder	171

List of Contributors

Dr. Jason McConnell is the Senior Pastor of the East Franklin Union Church and Franklin United Church in Franklin, VT. He also serves as co-director of the Ockenga Fellows Program and a Mentor in the Doctor of Ministry Program at Gordon-Conwell Theological Seminary.

Dr. David Horn was the Director of the Ockenga Institute at Gordon-Conwell Theological Seminary for over twenty years. He is currently the Executive Director of the Ockenga Fellows Program and a Mentor in the Doctor of Ministry Program at GCTS and serves as a Regional Director for InterVarsity Christian Fellowship.

Rev. Devon McCarley is a minister at Abundant Life Church in Cambridge, MA and the Director of Operations at the Emmanuel Gospel Center in Boston.

Rev. Joshua Cahan is the Senior Pastor of Ruggles Baptist Church in Boston.

Monica Roberts is the Youth Pastor at the Bethlehem Apostolic Holiness Faith Church of God in Boston and the Chief Engagement Officer for the Boston Public Schools.

Rev. Jonathan Romig is the Pastor of Cornerstone Congregational Church in Westford, MA.

Rev. Trip Weiler is the Pastor of Greenwoods Community Church in Ashley Falls, MA.

Jeff Miller is Professor of Theater Arts at Gordon College in Wenham, MA. Before coming to Gordon, Jeff served as the Chairman of the Theater Arts Department at Bethel University in St. Paul, MN.

Rev. Manny Daphnis is the Lead Pastor of Restoration Community Church in Brockton, MA.

List of Contributors

Rev. Tyler Smith is the Pastor of Georgia Plains Baptist Church in Georgia, VT.

Rev. Timothy Bogartman is the Senior Pastor of the First Congregational Church of Revere in Revere, MA.

Dr. Rick Harrington is the Lead Pastor of the First Baptist Church of Haverhill in Haverhill, MA.

Rev. David Coons is the Senior Pastor of Jericho Congregational Church in Jericho, VT.

Rev. Timothy Bresnahan is the Lead Pastor of Shipyard Church in Duxbury, MA.

Rev. Sean Roberts is the Senior Pastor of Christ the Redeemer Presbyterian Church in Portland, ME.

Rev. Canon Brian Bethke is the Canon Missioner for the Anglican Diocese in New England.

Dr. Ken Barnes is the Mockler-Phillips Professor of Workplace Theology and Business Ethics at Gordon-Conwell Theological Seminary. Dr. Barnes also serves as the Director of the Mockler Center for Faith and the Public Square and Co-Director of the Ockenga Fellows Program at GCTS.

Preface

I imagine that publishing a book is somewhat analogous to birthing a baby, but since I have done neither before, I can't really say for sure. I have, however, walked with my wife through four pregnancies and, therefore, know something about the simultaneous pain and pleasure a woman feels throughout this precarious process. As a coauthor and first-time general editor, I have experienced the exhilaration and exhaustion of watching an idea about a book on beauty and worship develop through all the gestations, from conception to delivery. Collaborating and cocreating with cherished colleagues (seventeen of us in all) spawned tremendous delight but being critiqued by each other caused moments of discomfort.

In the end, though, like a proud mother holding her beautiful newborn baby, I happily concede that the pleasure was worth the pain. I am, indeed, elated by each author's creativity and commitment to helping the Christian church see beauty, art, and worship in a different light.

This book was written by a cohort of pastors and scholars and college or seminary professors who participated in the Ockenga Fellows Program at Gordon-Conwell Theological Seminary from the fall of 2018 through the spring of 2020. This program, which is generously funded by the Lilly Endowment's Early Career Pastoral Leadership Development Initiative, creates cohorts of young clergy who explore issues of faith and ministry in the public square. Among other things, this cohort has toured key sites in New England's rich spiritual heritage, dialogued with faculty at Harvard Business School and the Boston College Lynch School of Education, met with legislators at the Massachusetts State House, walked on the Great Wall of China, and discovered artistic treasures displayed in the halls of the Boston Museum of Fine Arts together. What started out as a cohort of new acquaintances has now become a band of brothers and sisters. And now, we have accomplished the monumental task of publishing a book together!

This book has three primary purposes and audiences. First, the book is written for everyone who desires to think about art and beauty from a biblical, theological, and liturgical perspective. This book may serve as a resource for private worship and personal devotions. The chapters are neither long nor difficult to read, but they do provide a plethora of devotional ponderings (paintings, photographs, hymns, poems, songs, Scripture readings, theological reflections, and spiritual exercises) to help individuals worship our God in new ways. During the final editing phase, I read through the manuscript for my morning devotions while savoring copious cups of black coffee (which is an artistic and devotional endeavor in itself).

Second, this book could be used as an adult Sunday school or small group curriculum in a local church context. Again, the chapters are succinct enough that they can be read and discussed in little more than an hour's time. The "Discussion Questions" toward the end of each chapter are designed for this very purpose. Hopefully, this volume will stir the imagination of church members and spur them on toward greater expressions of artistic creativity in their own churches.

Third, this book may serve as a sermon source for pastors and a liturgical guide for church worship leaders. How interesting would it be for a pastor to shape this table of contents into an eighteen-week topical sermon series titled *Beholding Beauty*? Pastors, please feel free to use the theological reflections as starting points for sermons about worship and the arts. Modify them, expand them, contextualize them for your own church community, but by all means, preach them!

Likewise, how intriguing would it be for worship leaders to use the components in these chapters to form aesthetically invigorating church services? The calls to worship, hymns, poems, and liturgies are meant to arouse the soul in worship. But don't stop with these components; add your own creative elements to theologically coherent and compelling worship services. Challenge your congregation to not only contemplate our creative Creator with their minds, but to engage him with their eyes and ears and noses and tongues and hands and hearts. Use these pages as a launchpad to broaden and deepen your church's expressions of worship on Sunday mornings and special services throughout the church calendar.

And one more word about the book. You will notice that this volume does not cover a comprehensive list of the arts. The scope of this project wasn't large enough to accommodate chapters on fine arts such as architecture and opera or a host of worthy folk arts like quilting, woodworking, and taxidermy. I really wanted to include chapters on some of my personal favorites like classical music, whiskey distilling, and beer brewing, but to adapt the refrain of an old George Thorogood song, "One bourbon, one

Bach, and one beer. . .," overindulgence in anything, including art, usually leads to regret (and a headache) the next day.

In full disclosure, I even desired to include a chapter on the art of lovemaking. It seemed to me that a theological and aesthetic reflection on the erotic honeymoon scene in Song of Solomon 4 would be of great interest to married readers everywhere. I thought the potential for this chapter so profound that I even considered writing it myself, but alas, my winsome wife advised me against writing about topics where I lack the necessary knowledge and skill. Therefore, the arts that appear here must suffice until someone else comes along to compose a companion volume.

But there is a wide enough range of artforms in these pages for anyone to develop a deeper appreciation for God's beauty and the beauty he created in our world. There is also enough guidance for us to gain a greater sense of how we might utilize art and aesthetic to glorify God and enjoy him forever.

And finally, permit me to return to my birthing metaphor one last time. I must confess that serving as the general editor of a multi-author book is like a husband in the delivery room. Other people do the real work; you're just there to hold a hand and provide moral support along the way. It has been an honor and pleasure to share a birthing room with all of these authors from the beginning to the end of this venture! We hope this book will be as much of a blessing for you to read as it was for us to write! *Soli Deo Gloria*!

Jason McConnell
General Editor

Acknowledgments

We (the contributing authors) would like to thank Dr. Chris Coble, Vice President for Religion, and Dr. Jessica Duckworth, Program Director, at the Lilly Endowment Inc. and Rev. Libby Manning and Dr. Derek Nelson at the Wabash Pastoral Leadership Program. Your vision for the Resource Generation Grant in the Early Career Pastoral Development Initiative inspired this book project and made it possible.

We also express our gratitude to Gordon-Conwell Theological Seminary, which graciously hosted our Ockenga Fellows cohort from 2018–2020. This program will continue to bear fruit for the rest of our lives.

And last, but certainly not least, we would like to thank our families and the church communities we serve. Your constant love and support enable us to lead God's people in worship with creativity and imagination. You are an amazing expression of God's beauty in our lives.

Introduction
A Brief Reflection on Beauty and Longing

DAVID HORN

Lauterbrunnen (1863) by Alexandre Calame (1810–1864)

If beauty is something that has to be captured and contained in an experience, it happened about four years ago for me. Of course, I have experienced beauty many times in my life, but nothing like this. The two hours sitting on that outdoor patio in an old hotel in the ancient village of Murren, Switzerland—a village that hangs precariously on the side of the Lauterbrunnen Valley—chiseled beauty in stone for me. That moment is a monument to Beauty!

There were six of us on that patio, and we all experienced the same thing: We had all spent a week walking through the museums and concert halls of Vienna, and we were now experiencing the full splendor of what we had seen captured by the landscape paintings of the masters: various shades of light rushing across the rocky crags of the other side of the cavernous valley, set against the backdrop of a pallet of multi-shades of blue that was the sky. At times, clouds cried rain, but only briefly. The confluence of everything in that experience could not be described in any other way than that it was "beautiful": deep friendships, expressing heart-felt sentiments, set against the dramatic natural geography around us, in the midst of our long-drawn-out conversation on the nature of art and other more pedestrian ruminations. All played a part in the stunning beauty of that moment.

Central to beauty is a sense of transcendence that characterized our experience that day and, I suspect, more universally in all moments of beauty. As one aspect of the human experience, beauty stands out "like a sore thumb," as it were. Whereas much of our lives may be caught in the mundane, is it not the case that moments of beauty require our attention? They cannot be ignored. They stand apart and above anything else in our lives. It is in this sense that beauty is transcendent.

And it is for this reason that beauty is a much sought-after commodity in our lives. We crave beauty in the same way we crave transcendence. When it is not present, we seek after it to enfold us. When we do experience it, we delight in it, even for a moment. But even when we delight in beauty, is not part of that delight bittersweet? The transcendence of beauty is fleeting. The Romantics perhaps had it right; beauty is but for a moment, and efforts to capture the moment and store it away for a rainy day are futile.

It is the bittersweet nature of beauty that C. S. Lewis calls "longing." These two twin sisters—beauty and longing—are joined at the hip. Central to the nature of beauty is a sense of longing for something more. In *The Weight of Glory*, Lewis states,

> We do not want merely to see beauty, though, God knows, even that is bounty enough. We want something else which can hardly be put into words—to be united with the beauty we see, to pass into it, to receive it into ourselves, to bathe in it, to become part of it.[1]

1. Lewis, *Weight of Glory*, 12–13.

Introduction

Beauty, even as it is being displayed in what we see and hear and feel, evokes longing for more. A piece of great music compels us to desire an experience that is something more than what we are having. To see a great painting evokes a desire to see the larger world that it evokes. To hear the cadence of a great poem or feel the rising tension of a compelling story provokes longing in us that transcends the experience of beauty. To overlook the Grand Canyon and comprehend its magnitude demands something more in us. It may overwhelm us, but even as it does, it, strangely, leaves us longing for something more. In the most profound sense, the experience of beauty points to something larger than itself in all its forms.

For the Christian, the headwaters of this longing are not hard to find. It is found at the beginning of Scripture in the great litany of the story of Creation in Genesis 1 where we find the Creator's great declaration at the end of each day: "It was good." Embedded in each day is the beauty of goodness under the very fingernails of creation and—here is the amazing thing—some of that beauty still remains even after the Fall. The apostle Paul declares this residue of remaining goodness for what it is in Romans 8. He describes it as longing:

> The creation waits in eager expectation for the sons of God to be revealed. For the creation was subjected to frustration, not by its own choice, but by the will of the one who subjected it, in hope that the creation itself will be liberated from its bondage to decay and brought into the glorious freedom of the children of God. We know that the whole creation has been groaning as in the pains of childbirth right up to the present time. Not only so, but we ourselves, who have the firstfruits of the Spirit, groan inwardly as we wait eagerly for our adoption as sons, the redemption of our bodies (Rom 8:19–23).

We live in a fallen world, but beauty still abounds. It abounds, in part, as heart-felt groaning and under the guise of longing for something larger than what is easily experienced. Beauty still exists but is not easily found everywhere. It seeks transcendence and it is in the transcendence of God the Creator and Redeemer that Lewis finds the true source of beauty and our longing.

How is it that we find beauty in our world? Beauty all depends upon what we long for, and what we long for is what is at the heart of our desires. We return again to *The Weight of Glory* when Lewis declares,

> It would seem that our Lord finds our desire, not too strong, but too weak. We are half-hearted creatures, flailing about with drink and sex and ambition when infinite joy is offering us, like

an ignorant child who wants to go on making mud pies in a sum because he cannot imagine what is meant by the offer of a holiday at the sea. We are too easily pleased.[2]

What we define as beauty for ourselves depends upon where we cast our eyes, and our current state tends to long for all the wrong things. We look downward in the mud when we have an opportunity to look upward at the horizon. Beauty does exist in our world today, but where it doesn't, it most often is the result of looking and desiring for beauty in all the wrong places. Our perceptions are off; our expectations are wrong; the source of our desires is off-kilter. Beauty becomes distorted.

M.H. Abram's amazing critique of Romantic theory, *The Mirror and the Lamp*, indirectly speaks to the distortion we most often feel.[3] Abram makes the observation that Romantic sensibilities were a watershed moment in our history of perception. Prior to the nineteenth century, the artist looked outward to the natural world with the confidence that there was a concrete and relatively objective world. Even if the artist didn't see this objective world as the product of the divine, it at least pointed that way. After the Romantic period, the gaze of the artist looked inward as a basis for understanding their vision and forms.

Prior to the nineteenth century, the role of the artist was mimetic. The artist imitated with confidence what he or she could see. The beauty of a landscape painting, for example, was measured by how close it represented what the artist sought to imitate faithfully of the world around him or her. After the Romantic period, however, the reality of what was painted was measured subjectively from within. The artist defined what he or she saw and felt. Rather than the artist being one who held up a mirror to the world for all to see its beauty, the artist became his or her own lamp that illumined their own subjective vision of what he or she saw. What an amazing transformation of two different visions of the world.

Without saying anything about Abram's critical literary critique other than to use his two metaphors, beauty is no longer sought after by looking at the outside world and, potentially, at God. Beauty is now being defined by the artist him or herself. The ugly, the grotesque, the violent, and the mundane can now be passed off as beautiful. To use the words of W. B. Yeats in his poem "Easter Rising" to encapsulate the modern approach to beauty: "All changed, changed utterly. A terrible beauty is born." Beauty is what we want it to be. Or is it? In our current, modern sensibilities, what is lost is

---

2. Lewis, *Weight of Glory*, 1–2.
3. Abrams, *Mirror and the Lamp*, 57–60.

a sense of the transcendent, and a longing that no longer exists within the subjective vision of the artist.

All this leads us to the doorsteps of this little volume. What is worship? Worship clearly rests on the side of the mimetic vision, of pointing a mirror outward to something larger than ourselves. In worship, we have an opportunity to see the source of beauty in God the Creator and in Jesus our Redeemer and not in ourselves. Worship, at its core, is longing, longing for something—for Someone—beyond ourselves and our own human achievements. It transcends the mundane; it broadens our horizons; it offers us vast and eternal vistas; and it captures our imaginations if we allow it to. In so doing, it offers us a perspective on our lives that has the potential of bringing beauty back into our world in whole new ways.

Worship takes on many different forms, forms that you may not even have realized or exercised yourself. How does beauty that is expressed in the culinary arts, or in fragrance, or in the world of fashion, or fiction, or sculpture, or, heaven forbid, winemaking even, bring glory to God? They can! Buried deep in each is an element that has the potential of provoking longing in our souls for something more. I trust these pages will offer you a fresh vision of God and how he has made us, made in the image of God. If it would do so, that would be beautiful!

Chapter 1

God
The Original Artist

Jason McConnell

Creation of the Animals (c.1551) by Il Tintoretto

Jacopo Robusti—Il Tintoretto (1518–94) means "the little painter guy." A Venetian painter and draughtsman, and a representative of the school of mannerism, Il Tintoretto's work marked the transition between the Renaissance and Baroque periods. He was initially inspired by the work of

Michelangelo (1475–1564), but he soon developed a style of his own which utilized an array of vivid colors and dramatic contrasts between dark and light, a technique that would later be perfected by Caravaggio (1571–1610).

The horizontal lines in *The Creation of the Animals* flow from right to left in a whirling motion. In a blaze of golden light that pierces the darkness still enveloping the newly created earth, God the Father is suspended in mid-air during the act of creation. (Notice how this portrayal echoes Michelangelo's figure of God in the *Creation of Adam* in the Sistine Chapel painted forty years earlier.) The birds of the sky and fish of the sea rush forward on the fifth day while the land animals stand behind their creator, waiting in eager anticipation of the sixth day, when they would be unleashed to roam the earth. Il Tintoretto's luminous landscape scene captures the essence of God's artistry and creativity.

CALL TO WORSHIP (PSALM 8)

Leader: Lord, our Lord, how majestic is your name in all the earth. You have set your glory in the heavens.

People: Through the praise of children and infants you have established a stronghold against your enemies, to silence the foe and the avenger.

Leader: When I consider your heavens, the work of your fingers, the moon and the stars, which you have set in place,

People: What is mankind that you are mindful of them, human beings that you care for them?

Leader: You have made them a little lower than the angels and crowned them with glory and honor.

People: You made them rulers over the works of your hands; you put everything under their feet: all flocks and herds, and the animals of the wild, the birds in the sky, and the fish in the sea, all that swim the paths of the seas.

All: Lord, our Lord, how majestic is your name in all the earth!

HYMN "O GOD, THE JOY OF HEAV'N ABOVE" BY CHARLES COFFIN (1736)

O God, the joy of Heav'n above,
Thou didst not need Thy creatures' love,
When from Thy secret place of rest
Thy Word the earth's foundations blest.

Thou spakest: worlds began to be;
They bow before Thy majesty;
And all to their creator raise
A wondrous harmony of praise.

But ere, O Lord, this lovely earth
From Thy creative will had birth,
Thou in Thy counsels didst unfold
Another world of fairer mold.

That realm shall our Redeemer frame,
And build upon His mighty name;
His hand the word of power shall sow,
That all the earth His truth may know.

When time itself has passed away,
His Church, secure in Heav'n for aye,
Shall share His table and His throne,
And God the Father reign alone.

O Father, Son, and Spirit blest,
One God in Heav'n and earth confessed,
Preserve, direct, and fill with love
Thy realm on earth, Thy realm above.

SCRIPTURE READING (GENESIS 1)

In the beginning God created the heavens and the earth. Now the earth was formless and empty, darkness was over the surface of the deep, and the Spirit of God was hovering over the waters.

And God said, "Let there be light," and there was light. God saw that the light was good, and he separated the light from the darkness. God called the light "day," and the darkness he called "night." And there was evening, and there was morning—the first day.

And God said, "Let there be a vault between the waters to separate water from water." So God made the vault and separated the water under the vault from the water above it. And it was so. God called the vault "sky." And there was evening, and there was morning—the second day.

And God said, "Let the water under the sky be gathered to one place, and let dry ground appear." And it was so. God called the dry ground "land," and the gathered waters he called "seas." And God saw that it was good.

Then God said, "Let the land produce vegetation: seed-bearing plants and trees on the land that bear fruit with seed in it, according to their various kinds." And it was so. The land produced vegetation: plants bearing seed according to their kinds and trees bearing fruit with seed in it according to their kinds. And God saw that it was good. And there was evening, and there was morning—the third day.

And God said, "Let there be lights in the vault of the sky to separate the day from the night and let them serve as signs to mark sacred times, and days and years, and let them be lights in the vault of the sky to give light on the earth." And it was so. God made two great lights—the greater light to govern the day and the lesser light to govern the night. He also made the stars. God set them in the vault of the sky to give light on the earth, to govern the day and the night, and to separate light from darkness. And God saw that it was good. And there was evening, and there was morning—the fourth day.

And God said, "Let the water teem with living creatures, and let birds fly above the earth across the vault of the sky." So God created the great creatures of the sea and every living thing with which the water teems and that moves about in it, according to their kinds, and every winged bird according to its kind. And God saw that it was good. God blessed them and said, "Be fruitful and increase in number and fill the water in the seas, and let the birds increase on the earth." And there was evening, and there was morning—the fifth day.

And God said, "Let the land produce living creatures according to their kinds: the livestock, the creatures that move along the ground, and the wild animals, each according to its kind." And it was so. God made the wild animals according to their kinds, the livestock according to their kinds, and all the creatures that move along the ground according to their kinds. And God saw that it was good.

Then God said, "Let us make mankind in our image, in our likeness, so that they may rule over the fish in the sea and the birds in the sky, over the livestock and all the wild animals, and over all the creatures that move along the ground."

So God created mankind in his own image,
    in the image of God he created them;
        male and female he created them.

God blessed them and said to them, "Be fruitful and increase in number; fill the earth and subdue it. Rule over the fish in the sea and the birds in the sky and over every living creature that moves on the ground."

Then God said, "I give you every seed-bearing plant on the face of the whole earth and every tree that has fruit with seed in it. They will be yours for food. And to all the beasts of the earth and all the birds in the sky and all the creatures that move along the ground—everything that has the breath of life in it—I give every green plant for food." And it was so.

God saw all that he had made, and it was very good. And there was evening, and there was morning—the sixth day.

THEOLOGICAL REFLECTION

And God stepped out on space,
And he looked around and said:
I'm lonely—
I'll make me a world
And far as the eye of God could see
Darkness covered everything
Blacker than a hundred midnights
Down in a cypress swamp.
Then God smiled,
And the light broke,
And the darkness rolled up on one side,
And the light stood shining on the other,
And God said: That's good!
Then God reached out and took the light in his hands,
And God rolled the light around in his hands
Until he made the sun;
And he set that sun a-blazing in the heavens.
And the light that was left from making the sun
God gathered it up in a shining ball
And flung it against the darkness,
Spangling the night with the moon and stars.
Then down between
The darkness and the light
He hurled the world;
And God said: That's good!
Then God himself stepped down—

And the sun was on his right hand,
And the moon was on his left;
The stars were clustered about his head,
And the earth was under his feet.
And God walked, and where he trod
His footsteps hollowed the valleys out
And bulged the mountains up.
Then he stopped and looked and saw
That the earth was hot and barren.
So God stepped over to the edge of the world
And he spat out the seven seas—
He batted his eyes, and the lightnings flashed—
He clapped his hands, and the thunders rolled—
And the waters above the earth came down,
The cooling waters came down.
Then the green grass sprouted,
And the little red flowers blossomed,
The pine tree pointed his fingers to the sky,
And the oak spread out his arms,
The lakes cuddled down in the hollows of the ground,
And the rivers ran down to the sea;
And God smiled again,
And the rainbow appeared,
And curled itself around his shoulder.
Then God raised his arm and he waved his hand
Over the sea and over the land,
And he said: Bring forth! Bring forth!
And quicker than God could drop his hand,
Fishes and fowls
And beasts and birds
Swam the rivers and the seas,
Roamed the forests and the woods,
And split the air with their wings.
And God said: That's good!
Then God walked around,

And God looked around
On all that he had made.
He looked at his sun,
And he looked at his moon,
And he looked at his little stars;
He looked on his world
With all its living things,
And God said: I'm lonely still.
Then God sat down—
On the side of a hill where he could think;
By a deep, wide river he sat down;
With his head in his hands,
God thought and thought,
Till he thought: I'll make me a man!
Up from the bed of the river
God scooped the clay;
And by the bank of the river
He kneeled him down;
And there the great God Almighty
Who lit the sun and fixed it in the sky,
Who flung the stars to the most far corner of the night,
Who rounded the earth in the middle of his hand;
This Great God,
Like a mammy bending over her baby,
Kneeled down in the dust
Toiling over a lump of clay
Till he shaped it in his own image;
Then into it he blew the breath of life,
And man became a living soul.
Amen. Amen.

The American writer and civil rights activist James Weldon Johnson (1871-1938) published this poem titled "The Creation" in *The Book of American Negro Poetry* in 1922.[1] Johnson used a poetic style called "pulpit

1. Johnson, *Book of American Negro Poetry*, 71-73.

oratory" to retell the creation story from Genesis 1. This style, which incorporates vivid description and grandiose expression, is common in African-American rhetoric. It is a form of literary art that brings a story to life.

I love Johnson's poem—the imagery, the artistry, and the movement is marvelous—but I must dispute his assertion that God created the world because he was lonely. To the contrary, God has never experienced loneliness, nor is it even possible for him to do so. In the eternally self-existent triune Godhead, the persons of the Father, Son, and Holy Spirit have supreme relational fulfillment among themselves. God did not need to create the universe or angels or even human beings to satisfy some relational deficiency or emotional longing. He did not create the world because he was lonely; rather, he created it to display his glory and majesty (Ps 19:1)!

Apart from this unfortunate error, I think Johnson's poem is absolutely brilliant! It utilizes creative imagery and artistic expression to exhibit God's exquisite masterpiece. Johnson uses the potent art form of poetry to depict God, the original artist! This creative interpretation of Genesis 1 incites our imagination as we reconsider the creation story.

Creation Reconsidered: Science or Art?

Before we look at what Genesis 1 actually teaches us, let's consider what it does not teach, and hopefully avoid some mistakes well-intentioned people have made in the past. This text does not answer all of our questions about how or when the world came into existence. Even the iconic opening line of the Bible, "In the beginning, God created the heavens and the earth," (Gen 1:1) does not tell us when God created the universe. When we read this verse, we must ask ourselves, "In the beginning of what?" It is obviously not referring to the beginning of God and therefore, not the beginning of everything. Does the author mean something abstract like the beginning of time or history? Is it perhaps a more scientific beginning—like the beginning of matter or the universe? Or is it a simple literary summary that means "in the beginning of the story?"[2]

Notice, in verse 2, the creation story does not begin with the creation of matter; it begins with the cosmos already in existence, albeit in in a chaotic state: "The earth was formless and void, and darkness was over the face of the deep" (Gen 1:2). This verse raises several questions about creation: How did the earth become formless and void? Where did the darkness and the deep come from? The text simply does not answer these questions. We know from other places in Scripture that God created the universe out of

2. Walton, *Genesis*, 67.

nothing (Heb 11:3; Rev 4:11), but the author of Genesis begins the creation story with God bringing order out of chaos!

When the ancients wanted to describe creation, they had little interest in the material structure or formational history of the cosmos. Rather, their concerns focused on the functional cosmos. Genesis 1 was never intended to answer scientific questions like the Big Bang, the age of the earth, or even evolutionary process. When we reduce Genesis 1 to an apology for creation against evolution, we miss the whole point of the passage. Genesis 1 is not even primarily about creation; it is about the creator! It doesn't depict God as a cosmic scientist; it portrays him as the original artist!

The purpose of Genesis 1 is not to answer our scientific questions about how the world came to be; rather it is to affirm God as the original artist who transformed a chaotic cosmos into a picturesque planet where countless life forms could flourish. Therefore, let's shift our focus to what Genesis 1 actually teaches us about the creator. Allow me to highlight two simple truths we learn about this creative Creator: God is the original artist and he created human beings to be cocreators with him!

God, the Original Artist

The Bible begins, in the very first verse, by revealing God as the original artist. He conceived the complex universe in his imaginative mind and then spoke it into existence with incomparable craftsmanship. He created the heavens and the earth and everything within them. The story really begins in verse 2, when God brought order out of chaos. He brought form to the formless void—his breath was hovering over the surface of the deep and he spoke into the darkness and filled the empty and uninhabitable earth! Like a master sculptor who begins with a block of marble or lump of clay, God took the formless earth and fashioned it into a marvelous masterpiece. Like a piano virtuoso who arranges musical notes into melodious score, God arranged all of the pieces of the world to play in harmony together: day and night, sun and moon, birds and sky, fish and sea, mammals and land, and man and woman.

Throughout Genesis 1, we witness God's creative qualities and artistic abilities. His creation was not randomly or haphazardly thrown together; it was formed with intricate order and structure. There is a clear plan and a consistent pattern in the six days of creation. Do you see rhythm of creation? Each day begins with an announcement ("And God said"), and then a command ("Let there be"), separation ("and he separated"), a report ("and it was so"), a naming ("and God called"), an evaluation ("And God saw that it was good"), and finally a chronological marker ("and there was evening and morning").

The six days of creation are also divided into two triads, which contrast with the unformed and unfilled state of the earth when the story begins. On days one, two, and three, God created light, sky and sea, and land and vegetation. Then on days four, five, and six, God created the sun, moon, and stars to bear the light, fish to swim the seas and fowl to soar the skies, and livestock and wild animals to inhabit the land and eat the vegetation.

Like a Bach concerto or a great jazz composition, the original artist displayed a brilliant blend of unity and diversity in his creation. God brought order to the uninhabitable chaos and created this picturesque planet as a place for life to flourish. Therefore, every time you gaze upon the mountains and meadows, rocks and rivers, and forests and flowers, pause and appreciate the intricacies of the original artist! Whether it's the glimmer of a glorious sunrise shimmering across the sea or the alluring glow of a harvest moon hanging in the southern sky, the scent of balsam and fir while walking through the woods, the sweet taste of a ripe apple in autumn, or the sparrow singing her song in the bloomed dogwood, praise the original artist for his beauty and creativity! Every time you stroll through God's multi-dimensional art gallery, take time to reflect on his handiwork and thank him for such incredible gifts. And as you enjoy God's glorious creation, do your part to protect and preserve his marvelous masterpiece!

Created to Be Cocreators

As we consider God's artistic creativity through the first six days of creation, let's zoom in on the second part of the sixth day, the crescendo of creation, when God, the Holy Trinity, said, "Let us make man in our image, after our likeness. And let them have dominion over the fish of the sea and the birds of the heavens and over the livestock and over all the earth and over every creeping thing that creeps on the earth" (Gen 1:26). Like the other creatures, God created humans, male and female, with anatomical and reproductive diversity, so that they might perpetuate the human race. Then God commanded them to "Be fruitful and multiply and fill the earth and subdue it and have dominion." He created human beings to be creative—to take the raw materials he made and use them to create more human life and subdue the earth.

Since God created us to be cocreators with him, we uniquely reflect God's image and glory when we apply our creative abilities. God gave us the ability to create other human beings! He gave us the ability to subdue and exercise dominion over the earth by forging tools, erecting buildings, painting pictures, composing cantatas, crafting quilts, penning poems, telling stories, forming sculptures, baking cakes, shooting photographs, planting gardens, brewing beer, designing clothing, drawing blueprints, roasting coffee, choreographing dances, and making maple syrup. Consider two poignant quotes. The Nobel Prize-winning Russian author Aleksandr Solzhenitsyn once said,

> Another artist realizes that there is a supreme force above him and works gladly away as his apprentice under God's heaven… The artist is only given to sense more keenly than others the harmony of the world and all the beauty and savagery of the human contribution to it — and to communicate this poignantly to people. And even in the midst of failures and down at the very lower depths of existence — in poverty, prison, illness — the sensation of a stable harmony will never leave him.[3]

Likewise, the Austrian composer Joseph Haydn once noted,

> Never was I so devout as when I composed *The Creation*. I knelt down each day to pray to God to give me strength for my work… When I was working on *The Creation* I felt so impregnated with Divine certainty, that before sitting down to the piano, I would quietly and confidently pray to God to grant me the talent that was needed to praise Him worthily.[4]

We can live out Genesis 1 by joining Solzhenitsyn, Haydn, and the great cloud of artists who have glorified God by using their creative abilities to cocreate with him! What creative abilities has God given you? How are you using them to glorify God and bless other people around you? You never know how God might use even a modest work of art to inspire the masses! After all, God arranged the collaboration of a common Catholic priest (Father Josef Moore) and an ordinary elementary school teacher (Franz Gruber) to compose one of the world's most famous Christmas Carols "Silent Night!" Isn't it amazing how God's providence could orchestrate a forgotten poem and a simple guitar tune to teach the world about the birth of his son, our Savior, Jesus Christ?

---

3 Solzhenitsyn, "Art—for Man's Sake," *New York Times*.
4 Butterworth, *Haydn*, 122.

Conclusion

As we continue to reflect on God as the original artist and how we can cocreate with him, ponder this humorous yet profound quote from comedian Demitri Martin who once quipped, "The earth without art is just eh."

PRAYER

Eternal God, Creator of all that is seen and unseen, we worship you with all of our heart, soul, mind, and strength. You are, indeed, the divine and original artist. As you spoke the world into existence, you brought order out of chaos. You created time and space and filled your creation with all things bright and beautiful, all creatures great and small, all things wise and wonderful—yes Lord, you made them all! We praise you for your glorious creation and the many ways we can enjoy it. We humbly ask you to help us protect and preserve your handiwork.

O Lord, we thank you for creating human beings in your image and for giving us the capacity to cocreate with you. Help us discover and develop the artistic gifts that you have bestowed upon us so that we may glorify you and bless your people. In the name of the Father, the Son, and the Holy Spirit. Amen.

DISCUSSION QUESTIONS

1. From the largest galaxies to the smallest insects, God is the original artist who created everything in the universe. What are some of your favorite pieces of his art? How do you see God's beauty displayed in these creations?

2. What aspects of God's creation are being destroyed? What are some practical steps you can take to preserve God's glorious creation?

3. How does God's creating the earth out of a formless void and order out of chaos influence human art and ingenuity?

4. What artistic gifts has God given you? How do you us them to glorify God and bless others?

SPIRITUAL EXERCISES

1. Wake up before dawn, go outside, and watch the sunrise. Pay close attention to how the mounting light dispels the darkness. As the sun appears, watch how the colors change across the sky. Read Psalm 113:3 and reflect on its meaning. ("From the rising of the sun to the place where it sets, the name of the LORD is to be praised.")
2. Stay up late on a night when the sky is crystal clear. Lie down on a blanket and gaze up at the stars. Identify any planets or constellations you know. Count the stars until you can count no more. Consider your life compared to the vast universe. Pray Psalm 8:4 in your own words. ("What is mankind that you are mindful of them, human beings that you care for them?")
3. Go to one of your favorite places in nature (a mountaintop, the ocean, a forest, a river, a meadow of wildflowers, etc.) and admire God's handiwork: Gaze at the majestic scenery, listen to the subtle sounds, smell the fragrant aromas, taste any edible findings, and touch the various textures. Thank God for his beauty and creativity! Sing Cecil Frances Alexander's brilliant hymn "All Things Bright and Beautiful."
4. Spend a few hours strolling through an art gallery or museum. Identify some exhibits that appeal to you. Think about why you find some exhibits beautiful but not others. Also, pick a few diverse pieces and analyze the artist's craftsmanship. Consider how the artist brought order out of chaos. Offer a prayer of thanksgiving for God's gift of human creativity displayed through those particular pieces of art!

RESOURCES FOR FURTHER REFLECTION

1. *Walking on Water: Reflections on Faith and Art* by Madaline L'Engle
2. *Culture Care: Reconnecting with Beauty for Our Common Life* by Mokoto Fujimura
3. *Art and Faith: A Theology of Making* by Mokoto Fujimura and N.T. Wright
4. *For the Beauty of the Church: Casting a Vision for the Arts* by W. David O. Taylor
5. *It Was Good: Making Art to the Glory of God* by Ned Bustard
6. *The Art of God* by Ric Ergenbright

Chapter 2

Colorful Silence
The Art of Painting

Devon McCarley

On a Hill Far Away by Cornie D. McCarley

Cornie D. McCarley, my beloved father, was born in Buffalo, NY, in 1942. Throughout his life, he was a lover of the arts, producing home movies, designing sets, and painting. Cornie has been acknowledged on a variety of platforms for his ability to redefine visual art in the church. His expression of worship through the arts opened doors for many people to find their place in church and worship by elevating the gifts and talents God poured into each one of his creative designs.

His painting *On a Hill Far Away* was inspired by the story of Christ's crucifixion, where Jesus was nailed to a cross between two rebels. The bright colors behind the cross depict God's glory radiating through a backdrop of perpetual darkness and sin in the world. Just as the dove descended upon Jesus during his baptism, this scene represents God's love for his Son, in whom he is well pleased. This painting is an expression of God's love for us and his desire to use his gifts to display the aesthetic beauty of Christ amid the brokenness of the world.

CALL TO WORSHIP (I CORINTHIANS 2:1–8)

Leader: And so it was with me, brothers and sisters. When I came to you, I did not come with eloquence or human wisdom as I proclaimed to you the testimony about God.

People: For I resolved to know nothing while I was with you except Jesus Christ and him crucified.

Leader: I came to you in weakness with great fear and trembling. My message and my preaching were not with wise and persuasive words, but with a demonstration of the Spirit's power, so that your faith might not rest on human wisdom, but on God's power.

People: We do, however, speak a message of wisdom among the mature, but not the wisdom of this age or of the rulers of this age, who are coming to nothing.

Leader: No, we declare God's wisdom, a mystery that has been hidden and that God destined for our glory before time began.

People: None of the rulers of this age understood it, for if they had, they would not have crucified the Lord of glory.

HYMN "THE OLD RUGGED CROSS" BY GEORGE BENNARD (1912)

On a hill far away stood an old rugged cross
The emblem of suffering and shame
And I love that old cross where the dearest and best
For a world of lost sinners was slain

So I'll cherish the old rugged cross
Till my trophies at last I lay down
And I will cling to the old rugged cross
And exchange it some day for a crown

To the old rugged cross I will ever be true
Its shame and reproach gladly bear
Then he'll call me someday to my home far away
Where his glory forever I'll share

And I'll cherish the old rugged cross
Till my trophies at last I lay down
And I will cling to the old rugged cross
And exchange it some day for a crown

SCRIPTURE READING (MARK 15:33–39)

At noon, darkness came over the whole land until three in the afternoon. And at three in the afternoon Jesus cried out in a loud voice, *"Eloi, Eloi, lema sabachthani?"* (which means "My God, my God, why have you forsaken me?").

When some of those standing near heard this, they said, "Listen, he's calling Elijah."

Someone ran, filled a sponge with wine vinegar, put it on a staff, and offered it to Jesus to drink. "Now leave him alone. Let's see if Elijah comes to take him down," he said.

With a loud cry, Jesus breathed his last.

The curtain of the temple was torn in two from top to bottom. And when the centurion, who stood there in front of Jesus, saw how he died, he said, "Surely this man was the Son of God!"

THEOLOGICAL REFLECTION

In the motivational story *The Painter and His Master*, the narrator tells the tale of a young artist who had just completed his painting course and then took three days to paint a beautiful landscape. He wanted people's opinion about his caliber and painting skills. So, he exhibited his creation at a busy street corner, with a board that exhibited the following message below the easel, "I have painted this piece. Since I'm new to this profession, I might have made some mistakes in my strokes. Please put an 'X' wherever you see a mistake."

When he came back in the evening, he was shocked to see the whole canvas filled with crosses. Some people had even written their comments on the painting. Shattered and dejected, he ran to his master's home and burst into tears.

The young artist was breathing heavily, and his master overheard him saying, "I am useless! If this is how I've learned to paint, I'm not worth becoming a painter. People have rejected me completely. I feel like dying."

His master smiled and suggested, "My son, I will prove that you are a great artist and have learned how to paint wonderfully. Do as I say without questioning it. It will work!" The young artist reluctantly agreed and two days later, he presented a replica of his earlier painting to his master. His master took the painting and said gracefully, "Come with me."

Early in the morning, they arrived at the same street-crossing and displayed the same painting in exactly the same place. Now his master took out another board which read "Gentlemen, I have painted this piece. Since I'm new to this profession, I might have made some mistakes in my strokes. I have put a box with paint colors and brushes just below. Please do me a favor. If you see a mistake, kindly pick up the brush and correct it." Then the painter and his master walked back home.

Later that evening, when they returned to the street corner, the young painter was surprised to see there was not a single correction made. The next day they visited again, and found the painting remained untouched. And it is said that the painter and his master kept the painting on the street corner for a month and no corrections were made.[1]

In this story, the painter tried to find his place in the world and receive validation from a community that didn't understand his expression. As a result, the painter became discouraged with his work and questioned his

---

1 "Painter and His Master," *Motivational Stories*, http://storiesofmotivation.blogspot.com/2012/03/painter-and-his-master.html.

calling—until his master taught him an important lesson about criticism, confidence, and contentment in art.

Likewise, at some point in their journey, most artists have faced these same questions, "Where do I fit in?" and "Am I good enough?" Even artists need to be reminded that they are created in the image of God and bear the same creative attributes as the Creator. When artists question their ability and calling, they would benefit from learning that they fit in through the redemptive work of the cross and their skills are already sacred and are being sanctified.

Through the cross, everything that God created is in the process of being restored to its original beauty. Every human being, along with their talents and gifts, is being redeemed by the blood that dripped from the Savior's brow; painfully, yet poetically painting a picture of salvation.

When God creates artists, he endows them with a unique aptitude to illuminate his truth and beauty. A painter has the ability to speak through forms and colors. And this colorful silence displays God's glory to the watching world. In John 12:32, Jesus says, "And I, when I am lifted up from the earth, will draw all people to myself."

Indeed, it is easy to criticize someone else's work, especially when we don't have the ability to do it ourselves. But when we are challenged to correct the mistake, we are in a better position to appreciate the incredible skill that goes into a particular craft. After all, what someone may view as a mistake, someone else may see as a masterpiece. So, I invite you to journey with me to the moment when God removed all the X's from your canvas and consider Christ's love revealed through colorful silence.

The Colors of Beauty

It was the ninth hour and darkness eclipsed the land. Can you see various shades of black obscuring the sun and dimming the hearts of those who loved him? Can you see the multicolored garments among the multitude of onlookers who came to see the spectacle? Can you see the centurion's bronze shield shimmering boldly against the torch's auburn glow? Can you see the brazen smirks under the Pharisee's long brown beards? Can you see the tawny thorns twisted around the crown pressing into Jesus's head? Can you see the iron nails holding his hands and feet in place? Can you see the purple bruises dotting his dirty olive skin? Can you see his limp form hanging from the tree—pale flesh and face stained with crimson blood? And can you hear the deafening silence in the air after he whispered the words, "My God, my God, why have you forsaken me?" before he breathed his final breath.

We often turn away from the cruel colors of the cross—they're too gruesome, too uncomfortable, too disturbing to behold—because we know that it was our sin that painted this appalling picture. Yet, if we stare into the darkness long enough, beauty begins to emerge. But how can beauty be veiled behind the darkness of the cross? Where can we find beauty in a bludgeoned body? How can beauty arise from the shadows of death? Death is beautiful when it pays the penalty for sin and offers hope to helpless sinners like us! As night is darkest just before dawn, death is most beautiful when it foreshadows the hope of resurrection! Look into the depths of this canvas, filled with the colors of death and life, and behold the glory of God—the glory that God receives when mankind is reconciled to the Father.

The painter's hand can transport us to a place of remembrance and repentance. And this image of Christ on the cross is a collection of a thousand unspoken words etched into our hearts and will remain there forever. As the painter carefully strokes the canvas, the painting portrays the words of Christ. It tells the story of how Christ died for us.

Our identity is found in Jesus's death on the cross. Sin was our identity, but through Christ's work on the cross, he redeemed our souls and began the process of restoring us to our original beauty. With strokes from the artists's hand, the gospel of Jesus Christ is captured and released. Just as Christ's last breath brought saving light into the world, so his redeeming power buys back the canvas, the paint, and the brush that a painter uses to worship God and bring him glory. This painting, silently yet powerfully, displays victory over the darkness. Even the centurion caught a glimpse of God's glory when he acknowledged "Truly this Man was the Son of God!" (Mk 15:39).

The Colors of Piety

Artists are called to use their gifts to exhibit God's beauty and truth to the world, but they cannot do this apart from time spent in private and corporate worship. Artists cannot depict beauty until they bask in beauty. But devotion is experienced beyond words on a page. If you look deeply into a painting, it displays the medium, but also the meditation, the prayers, and the piety of the painter. The famous French painter, Oscar Claude Monet once said, "What keeps my heart awake is colorful silence." The ability to paint what one has received out of a time of devotion is like a minstrel becoming one with their instrument in song or as a preacher developing a sermon through deep study and prayer.

What keeps the heartbeat of a painter is the ability to create a painting and let it speak the truth divulged from intimate whispers of prayer. Mary

Oliver concludes her poem "Upstream" with the poignant observation, "attention is the beginning of devotion."[2] Painters pay attention to details; not just with the strokes of a brush, but every stroke lived for Jesus Christ.

Paintings are not only developed from devotion, but they are also an act of devotion—a spiritual discipline where the painter listens, searches, and expresses the heart of God. When a painting is created from a place of piety, it intersects emotions and experiences from the past, present, and future in one moment of time and opens the door of heart to receive love and truth.

As you admire the painter's work, he or she is offering you a window into their own soul. They are sharing their devotion with you. Do you see it? Do you see the painter's place in the kingdom of heaven?

God created the painter's hands to capture everything in his great creation. These hands are not meant to be hidden. The hands that a painter lifts up to God are the same hands that put in color God's love for this world, especially humanity. There are no words that can truly express the greatness of God. When there are no words, the orator steps aside and allows the painter to add hues of color to a canvas, capturing what words cannot. Even the mundane becomes marvelous!

When you shout the word "Calvary" there is an image that automatically follows, and we are transported to the place where our Lord was crucified. It is the painter's call to seize within the edges of their canvas all of what Christ's death on the cross meant, and the gift of life it brings to those who hear its call.

Painting can speak God's voice and make it come alive in ways that words cannot. On the cross, Jesus's silence screamed aloud the forgiveness of sin. Jesus's physical words, ". . .forgive them for they know not what they do" are stamped "finished" when he closed his eyes and breathed his last breath. This colorful silence is displayed through a darkness that filled the earth the day Christ died. Yet, amidst the darkness there was a light piercing through; a light that darkness could not comprehend or overcome.

The purpose of painting is to illustrate God's beauty amid a broken world. Sometimes the painter draws our attention to the beauty, other times the brokenness. And every so often, the painter even captures broken beauty. When painters commune with the Creator and then put their brushes to the canvas, they become the mouthpieces of God, declaring his truth and beauty, in colorful silence.

---

2. Quoted in Foer, "Attention is the Beginning," *The Atlantic*, https://www.theatlantic.com/technology/archive/2019/05/mary-olivers-poetry-captures-our-relationship-technology/589039/.

Conclusion

My father often tells the story of his lifelong struggle with academics. Growing up, his peers mocked him for the amount of time he needed to grasp a particular subject matter. When he was young, Grandma Ida (his mother) explained to him that before he was born, when she was in labor at the hospital, the nurses tried to delay the delivery until the doctor arrived. As a result, Grandma Ida had always felt that this refusal to let her son be born may have caused the learning difficulties he faced most of his life. Cornie McCarley was ready to come into the world, but he was continually held back until the appropriate people arrived.

However, despite his consistent troubles in school with typical subjects like math and reading, my dad noticed that he possessed some natural talent in the arts. In a world where he often asked the question, "Where do I fit in?," he began to realize that his life could not be constricted to a place of black and white, but he needed a world with a full expression of vibrant colors. "God gave me the gift of art and music," he said, and it was this creative ability that brought a sense of purpose into young Cornie's life.

When we fix our eyes and tune our ears to the gifts God has given us, we can catch a vision for who God created us to be and what God created us to do. Just as the eagle flaps its wings to fly and flowers expand their petals to bloom, God created all of his good creation to worship him. And as the artist paints on an empty canvas, so it is true worship.

Worship is a lifestyle requiring a life full of devotion to God. Allow yourself to hear the words from heaven and respond to God with the unique expression he placed in you. You are God's handiwork, created in Christ Jesus for good works, which God prepared beforehand that you should walk in them. Remember that you were fearfully and wonderfully made; use the talents and gifts God has given you to fearfully and wonderfully cocreate with him!

If you are a painter, paint to the glory of God! May your handiwork preach God's truth so observers may behold God's beauty! If you are not a painter, open your eyes and gaze upon a variety of colorful canvases and appreciate their aesthetic beauty! Contemplate these expressions of colorful silence! They may seem abstract at times but ponder the art and the artist. Open your mind and heart to the emotions and viewpoints of a painting. Partner with an artist to develop a richer understanding of its meaning. And even though you may never fully understand the creation or the creator, you can still stand together and worship God through the art of painting.

PRAYER

Father, I thank you for your death on the cross. I thank you for your redeeming power that restored mankind and for the creative gifts you have bestowed upon us. Lord, help me to use my mind and hands for your glory. Help me to appreciate painters and paintings that transform an empty canvas into a rainbow of colors that testify to your truth and love.

May I always find my identity in Jesus Christ and his sacrifice on the cross. May the rich love of a Holy God make room for me as I find myself standing before the Most High with the lifted work of my hand.

Thank you for who you are and the reminder that if I am uniquely gifted in my work, I will rise and be promoted. I will not be held back as you will have me to stand before kings; not for idolatrous purposes but that you receive the glory and the honor and all the praise. May the words from my mouth and the mediation of my heart be acceptable in your sight, O Lord, my Rock, and my Redeemer. Amen.

DISCUSSION QUESTIONS

1. Who are some of your favorite painters? What do you like about them? How does their particular form and style speak to you?
2. How does the everyday working artist fit into God's plan for the world? As we are called to glorify God, what does that look like in practical application, as one pursues painting?
3. How can you glorify God through your art? How can art help you grow in your devotion to God?
4. How can the visual arts be incorporated into the life and worship of your church community? How can your church "create space" for artists to exhibit their artistic expressions of worship?

SPIRITUAL EXERCISES

1. Take a trip to one of the world's great art galleries like the Louvre in Paris, the National Gallery in London, or the Metropolitan Museum of Art in New York City. Gaze upon some of the great biblical paintings from masters like Da Vinci, Rembrandt, and Caravaggio. Ponder how

their brush strokes bring the great biblical narratives to life. Imagine what it would have been like to live in the scene that is depicted.

2. Purchase a graphic art daily devotional book such as Jane William's *The Art of Advent: A Painting a Day from Advent to Epiphany*. Read the entry and look at the painting for each day. Personalize and pray through the theological content revealed in each painting.

3. Organize a trip to a local art gallery for a group from your church. Give everyone time to choose one painting that captures their imagination. Then view each piece that was chosen and ask the person to explain why they chose that particular piece. Interpret the piece as a group and discuss how it displays truth and beauty.

4. Host a "graphic art gallery" night at your church. Invite artists from your church and/or community to exhibit and explain a piece of their artwork. Give time for questions, discussion, and theological reflection.

RESOURCES FOR FURTHER REFLECTION

1. *Art for God's Sake: A Call to Recover the Arts* by Philip Graham Ryken
2. *Visual Faith—Art, Theology, and Worship in Dialogue* by William A. Dyrness
3. *Sanctifying Art: Inviting Conversation Between Artists, Theologians, and the Church* by Deborah Sokolove
4. *Upstream: Selected Essays* by Mary Oliver

Chapter 3

The Divine Sculptor
The Art of Sculpture

Joshua Cahan

Hand of God (c.1907) by François Auguste René Rodin

The Divine Sculptor

Considered the founder of modern sculpture, François Auguste René Rodin was born into a working-class family in Paris, France in 1840. He was predominately self-educated, though studied drawing and painting at the Petite École and later took classes with animal sculptor Antoine-Louis Barye. Rodin was especially inspired by the work of Michelangelo. He is best known for *The Thinker*, a massive bronze figure which has come to represent philosophy.

However, in 1896, Rodin modeled the above, lesser-known work, which is found in both bronze and marble, entitled, *The Hand of God*. He presents the creation act of God as that of the skillful hand of the sculptor. Notice the contrast of the polished right hand of the divine sculptor exploding out of the rough, unformed rock. The divine sculptor is depicted as powerfully forming yet gently cradling Adam and Eve, who are entwined together in the fetal position.

CALL TO WORSHIP (EPHESIANS 2:8-10, 19-22)

Leader: For by grace you have been saved through faith.

People: And this is not your own doing; it is the gift of God, not a result of works, so that no one may boast.

Leader: For we are his workmanship, created in Christ Jesus for good works, which God prepared beforehand, that we should walk in them.

People: Consequently, you are no longer foreigners and aliens, but fellow citizens with God's people and members of God's household, built on the foundation of the apostles and prophets, with Christ Jesus himself as the chief cornerstone.

Leader: In him the whole building is joined together and rises to become a holy temple in the Lord.

People: And in him you too are being built together to become a dwelling in which God lives by his Spirit.

HYMN "HAVE THINE OWN WAY, LORD" BY ADELAIDE A. POLLARD (1906)

Have thine own way, Lord!
Have thine own way!
Thou art the potter, I am the clay.
Mold me and make me after thy will,
while I am waiting, yielded and still.

Have thine own way, Lord!
Have thine own way!
Search me and try me, Savior today!
Wash me just now, Lord, wash me just now,
as in thy presence humbly I bow.

Have thine own way, Lord!
Have thine own way!
Wounded and weary, help me I pray!
Power, all power, surely is thine!
Touch me and heal me, Savior divine!

Have thine own way, Lord!
Have thine own way!
Hold o'er my being absolute sway.
Fill with thy Spirit till all shall see
Christ only, always, living in me!

SCRIPTURE READING (ISAIAH 64:1–12)

Oh, that you would rend the heavens and come down,
 that the mountains would tremble before you!
  As when fire sets twigs ablaze
   and causes water to boil,
  come down to make your name known to your enemies
   and cause the nations to quake before you!
 For when you did awesome things that we did not expect,
  you came down, and the mountains trembled before you.
 Since ancient times no one has heard,
  no ear has perceived,
 no eye has seen any God besides you,
  who acts on behalf of those who wait for him.
 You come to the help of those who gladly do right,
  who remember your ways.
 But when we continued to sin against them,
  you were angry.
   How then can we be saved?
 All of us have become like one who is unclean,

and all our righteous acts are like filthy rags;
we all shrivel up like a leaf,
    and like the wind our sins sweep us away.
No one calls on your name
    or strives to lay hold of you;
for you have hidden your face from us
    and have given us over to our sins.
Yet you, Lord, are our Father.
    We are the clay, you are the potter;
    we are all the work of your hand.
Do not be angry beyond measure, Lord;
    do not remember our sins forever.
Oh, look on us, we pray,
    for we are all your people.
Your sacred cities have become a wasteland;
    even Zion is a wasteland, Jerusalem a desolation.
Our holy and glorious temple, where our ancestors praised you,
    has been burned with fire,
    and all that we treasured lies in ruins.
After all this, Lord, will you hold yourself back?
    Will you keep silent and punish us beyond measure?

THEOLOGICAL REFLECTION

Imagine you're a sculptor looking up at a sixteen-foot-tall, twelve-ton block of marble towering over you. You've been commissioned to make a larger-than-life sculpture for the cathedral of Florence, Italy. But as you look closer at the slab, you notice that it is full of "taroli," or vein-looking imperfections and cavities that are not only ugly but could also threaten the stability of the statue. Do you see the beauty of what this imperfect block of marble could be, putting your skill and reputation on the line, or do you decline the commission in search of a more suitable material to display your creativity?

This is the question that one of the history's greatest sculptors faced in the summer of 1501. The unappealing block of veined marble had sat untouched in a courtyard in Florence for decades. Other prominent artists had rejected it due to its imperfections, but finally one sculptor took on the commission to carve beauty out of this humble slab. Working in secrecy over a two-year period, this skilled sculptor transformed the formerly rejected and flawed block of marble into the towering and breathtaking masterpiece that so many recognize today: Michelangelo's *David*. Could you imagine being present for the dramatic unveiling in January 1504 to see this incredible creative work by one of the greatest artists in the world?

In Isaiah 64, he prophesies that the nation of Israel will rebel against their maker and consequently, they will be conquered by the Babylonians and taken into captivity. But in this same chapter, Isaiah cries out for mercy and deliverance on behalf of God's people. Near the conclusion of this passionate prayer, he portrays Israel as humble material made weak and ugly by the deep "taroli" of sin, but he depicts God as the Divine Sculptor—the potter looking down at his clay (verse 8). The great reformer John Calvin wrote, "Wisdom consists almost entirely of two parts: the knowledge of God and of ourselves."[1] So, what can we learn about God from his self-revelation as the Great Sculptor? What can we learn about ourselves?

The Father/Sculptor Connection

First, we see that the image of God as artist is connected to the much more prevalent image of God as Father. In fact, in the poetic structure of the Israelites's prayer, Father and artist are placed in parallel. Throughout Scripture, these images are often married as God the Father is identified by his creative works. 1 Corinthians 8:6 says, "For us there is one God, the Father, from whom are all things and for whom we exist." And Malachi 2:10, "Have we not all one Father? Has not one God created us?"

The reality of God's creation power is not impersonal but personal. We should not mistake the Divine Sculptor image as portraying God as removed personally from his creatures, though the difference is great as we will see below. The Apostle Paul casts our eyes toward creation to "clearly perceive" God's "invisible attributes, namely, his eternal power and divine nature" (Romans 1:20). And, of course, the Lord formed humanity in his own image and after his likeness (Genesis 1:27). "The God who made the world and everything in it. . .gives to all mankind life and breath and everything. And he made from one man every nation of mankind to live on all the face of the earth. . .that they should seek God, and perhaps feel their way toward him and find him. Yet he is actually not far from each one of us" (Acts 17:24, 25–27).

Yet this connection of Fatherhood to creation refers not only to the general act toward humanity but of God's saving work—forming a special people miraculously through his loving covenant with Abraham, rescuing his people from slavery in Egypt, and preparing for them to enter the Promised Land. On the cusp of entering this land, Moses reminded God's people:

1. Calvin, *Institutes*, 4.

"Is not he your father, who created you, who made you and established you? ...When the Most High gave to the nations their inheritance, when he divided mankind, he fixed the borders of the peoples according to the number of the sons of God. But the Lord's portion is his people, Jacob his allotted heritage" (Deut 32:6b, 8–9). This special relationship is reinforced both in the beginning and ending of Isaiah's prayer. At the start, he acknowledges God as Father in the hopes of "stirring [His] inner parts and [His] compassion" toward his people (Isa 63:16), and at the conclusion, he appeals to God on behalf of Israel as his special people: "Behold, please look, we are all *your people*" (Isa 64:9, emphasis added).

This Father/Sculptor connection is good news. An all-powerful creator God is only good news if he is benevolent, if he can be trusted, if he loves us. Praise God that he is not only our creator but also our Father. Praise God that he didn't just mold our bodies, but he breathed life into us! Praise God that, as Jesus said, even as evil earthly fathers love and bless their children, how much more does your Father in heaven love you and delight in you (Matt 7:11)!

Indeed, sculptors—and artists generally—truly put themselves into their work. It's as much "begetting" as working. Michelangelo labored tirelessly for two years to sculpt his famous *David*. Since he worked in the open courtyard when it rained he was often soaked. His biographer Ascanio Condivi (1525–74) wrote that during these two years Michelangelo ate and slept only sporadically, and when he did make time to rest, he slept in his clothes, and even with his boots, still on.

When sculptors/artists pour themselves into their work, they are reflecting both the skill and love of the Divine Sculptor, our Father, who chisels and shapes us with passion and love. Consider your own profession for a moment. Have you thought about how putting yourself into your work brings God glory? Being both a skillful and loving software engineer or bus driver or physician's assistant reflects the creative power and love of our Father.

The Potter/Clay Distinction

Nevertheless, the relational emphasis in the Father/Sculptor connection should not minimize the great chasm of power and authority that lies between God and man. This picture of the Potter and the clay highlights the incredible distinction between the Sculptor and stone.

This image of God as Potter and his people as clay is most commonly associated with the unlimited sovereignty of God over his people. The prophet Jeremiah, writing later than Isaiah but in the similar context of

Israel's rebellion and God's judgment employs this imagery in a shocking way: "I went down to the potter's house, and there he was working at his wheel. And the vessel he was making of clay was spoiled in the potter's hand, and he reworked it into another vessel, as it seemed good to the potter to do. Then the word of the Lord came to me: 'O house of Israel, can I not do with you as this potter has done?'" (Jer 18:3–5).

In his letter to the Romans, the apostle Paul echoes Jeremiah when wading through the deep waters of God's sovereignty over salvation. When Paul, through rhetorical questions, arrives at the heart of the paradox of God's sovereign power of salvation and human responsibility to believe, he turns to the image of the divine sculptor: "Who are you, O man, to answer back to God? Will what is molded say to its molder, 'Why have you made me like this?' Has the potter no right over the clay, to make out of the same lump one vessel for honorable use and another for dishonorable use?" (Rom 9:20–21). Indeed, this image reminds us that God is unlike us in substance and authority and power. It is a miracle that we can relate to God and that God has stamped his image on us, but there is much bad theology that flows from the subtle assumption that God is just a super-human. No, he is completely other!

Sculptors not only reflect this same fatherly care in their work but also the enormous chasm between maker and made. Michelangelo's *David* began simply as a low-quality block of marble. The slab's life and beauty is entirely dependent on the active work of the great artist. The sculptor's mastery of the stone or the potter's control of the clay reflects God's complete sovereignty over us. And indeed, how much greater is the gap between the eternal, uncreated God, and us! So often we view God as simply a super-human—a bigger and more powerful version of ourselves. But God is wholly other, completely different from us. What are the implications of God's transcendence above us?

First, it should bring context to our tendency to grasp for power in politics and culture. God is not so small that he needs us to protect Him. No, "the king's heart is a stream of water in the hand of the Lord; he turns it wherever he will" (Prov 21:1). And we have confidence that one day *every* knee will bow before Jesus as Lord (Phil 2:10).

Second, this emphasis on God's sovereignty is a reminder of the way of Jesus. The journey of discipleship is the narrow, difficult road (Matt 7:13–14) of repentance. Even though the primary call of the world around us says we should "treat yourself" or "be yourself" or "love yourself," the call of Jesus is to *deny* yourself, to acknowledge him as Lord and submit to his word and ways.

Third, it should be a comfort to us. The sovereign power of God first strikes us as uncomfortable. To admit it is to acknowledge your lack of control. And yet as you reflect more and more, the knowledge that the divine sculptor is sovereignly sustaining us is incredibly comforting, especially in times of trial and uncertainty when you're reminded of how little control you really have over your life.

The Justice/Mercy Question

This final insight from God revealing himself as Sculptor gets to Isaiah's purpose in employing the imagery in his prayer. Back in verse 5, Isaiah praises the powerful activity of the Lord on behalf of his people: "You meet him who joyfully works righteousness, those who remember you in your ways." But then he immediately acknowledges Israel's reality. Israel would rebel against God by worshiping idols, oppressing the poor, and even practicing child sacrifice. Verse 7 sums up this reality: "There is no one who calls upon your name, who rouses himself to take hold of you; for you have hidden your face from us and have made us melt in the hand of our iniquities." Do you hear the contradiction? God works on behalf of those who trust in him, and yet Israel had been unfaithful to the Lord over and over again with no sign of repentance. It is this conflict that leads Isaiah to conclude his prayer with a climactic question: "Will you keep silent, and afflict us so terribly?" (verse 12).

Here we see the thrust of how Isaiah uses this Divine Sculptor image in the context. Will the Artist simply toss aside the work on which he has lavished care and attention, into which he has put so much of Himself? Isaiah appeals to God: although our sin cannot be denied, neither can our relationship with you. Yes, we are like dry and moldy clay, but we are *yours*. This of course gets to the central problem in all of Scripture: How can a just God show mercy to sinful people?

This question leaves us searching for an answer that ultimately comes in the New Testament through the person and work of Jesus Christ. Jesus, the perfect image of the invisible God, who is both the Creator and the firstborn Son of all creation, the One in whom the fullness of God was pleased to dwell, came to bring reconciliation between God and man, made peace by the blood of his cross (Col 1:15–20). The compelling question of Isaiah's prayer was answered when God's justice and mercy collided on the cross—Jesus satisfied God's judgment and reconciled sinners with their Creator. This is the gospel, the good news, that whoever believes and receives Jesus as Lord and Savior will be saved. They will be renewed and raised from the grave just as Jesus was to live in eternal bliss with their Creator. But the good news of Jesus is not only about securing our eternal future. The Spirit of Christ transforms our hearts, molding us and shaping us as his *new* creation as we walk in the good works he has prepared for us (Eph 2:10). What amazing grace!

In the early morning of September 13, 1501, when Michelangelo first began carving this marble slab full of "taroli," he could have followed in the footsteps of the sculptors before him and rejected the commission, calling the material an expensive lost cause. But out of love and sacrifice, he persevered. The imperfections were a huge impediment. In fact, *David* took so much time to complete partially because Michelangelo needed to use a lime mortar to fill and cover up the ugly imperfections and cavities in order to stabilize the structure. And before the unveiling of *David* in 1504, Michelangelo spent months polishing its surface to beautify and reinforce his masterpiece with a weather-resistant patina. Giorgio Vasari, a 16th century biographer, would later describe Michelangelo's work as "the bringing back to life of one who was dead."[2]

Isn't that like what God has done for you? Though he could have thrown out his spoiled material, the divine sculptor persevered in life-changing love and power, sacrificing even Himself in order to bring us to new life. What a God we worship!

PRAYER

Dear Lord, thank you for revealing yourself as the divine sculptor. Open my eyes to see and my heart to find comfort in the pillow of your sovereignty, especially in times of uncertainty. Guard me from thinking of you only as a glorified version of myself. Help me to see the joy in submission to you.

May I also remember that your creative power is intimately connected to your Fatherly love for me—that you delighted to birth me and to re-birth me through your Holy Spirit. Would you help me to work out my salvation, willing and acting according to your good pleasure? May I walk in in the good works you have prepared for me as you continue to mold and shape me as your handiwork.

DISCUSSION QUESTIONS

1. What are some of your favorite sculptures? Why do you like them?

2. Britannica, "How a Rejected Block", para 4.

2. Isaiah 64 teaches that God is both like us, as a Father to his children, and unlike us, as a Potter to his clay. Christian theologians call this the immanence (or intimate closeness) and transcendence (or ruling power) of God. In your relationship with God, do you approach him more as an intimate friend or sovereign ruler? Why is it important to balance these two perspectives of God as we relate with him?

3. The Father/Sculptor connection emphasizes our own likeness with God, who made us to reflect his own creative power in our lives. How does your work reflect the creative power of your Creator?

4. Scripture's emphasis on God's limitless sovereignty in the Potter/clay distinction can make us feel uncomfortable. But why should this comfort us?

5. Share how God has chiseled you and filled in the "taroli" in your life. Looking back, in which specific areas do you notice his creative transformation?

SPIRITUAL EXERCISES

1. Start a book club using one of the resources below—either with fellow church members for spiritual growth or with neighbors outside the church for evangelism.

2. Enroll in a pottery class or workshop with some other church members. Take time afterward to discuss what insights you gained about the Lord as Sculptor.

3. Gather some church members and take a guided tour of a local museum's sculpture exhibit or a local sculpture park. You could also ask a sculpture artist to give you a tour and explanation of his or her work. If the artist is a Christian you can ask about how they connect their faith with their art.

4. Read Isaiah 64 for your family devotional time and teach your children about God as Divine Sculpture using play dough.

RESOURCES FOR FURTHER REFLECTION

1. *Clay in the Potter's Hands* by Diana Pavlac Glyer
2. *The Giant: A Novel of Michelangelo's David* by Laura Morelli

3. *Shaping the World: Sculpture from Pre-history Until Now* by Antony Gormley and Martin Gayford
4. The Center for Christianity, Culture, and the Arts at Biola University, particularly lecture 1 by sculptors Tom Tsuchiya, Lynn Aldrich, and John Leighton

Chapter 4

Adequately Clothed
The Art of Fashion

MONICA ROBERTS

God's Curse, Adam And Eve (c.1896–1902) by James Tisso

French painter, James Jacques Joseph Tissot was born in Nantes, France in 1836, and studied at Ecole des Beaux-Arts in Paris. His first exhibition was at the age of twenty-three in the Paris Salon. Tissot's early work focused on French history, but by the late 1800s, he painted scenes from social events. Before his death, he became a devout man out of which was born his biblically referenced art.

God's Curse, Adam and Eve transports the viewer to a moment of moments. With lowered heads, Adam and Even stand overcome with shame, aware of their nakedness and sin, and perhaps afraid as their maker called out to them. The aprons covering over their reproductive parts may be a nod to the association with lust and sensuality that would come thereafter. Covered with leaves, Eve symbolizes the feeble attempt made to clothe the human body. This is juxtaposed with Adam covered with animal skin—the first animal sacrifice made for man. Despite being birthed as the result of sin, fashion has a place and purpose in glorifying God.

CALL TO WORSHIP (GALATIANS 3:22–27)

Leader: But the Scripture declares that the whole world is a prisoner of sin, so that what was promised, being given through faith in Jesus Christ, might be given to those who believe.

People: Before the coming of this faith, we were held in custody under the law, locked up until the faith that was to come would be revealed.

Leader: So, the law was our guardian until Christ came that we might be justified by faith. Now that this faith has come, we are no longer under a guardian.

People: So, in Christ Jesus you are all children of God through faith, for all of you who were baptized into Christ have clothed yourselves with Christ.

HYMN "TAKE OFF THE OLD COAT" BY JOHNSON OATMAN JR. (1898)

The feast is prepared, you're urged to come in,
Long years you have worn that old coat of sin;
But for such a feast this old garment won't do,
Then take off the old coat, put on the new.

Refrain
O take off the old coat, put on the new,
For Christ has a garment ready for you;
White robes of salvation wait at the door,
Then take off the old coat, wear it no more.

The old coat has brought you sorrow and care,
It led you to shame, it led to despair;
It never has been a blessing to you,
Then take off the old coat, put on the new.

The old coat is soiled, without and within,
All covered with guilt, all spotted with sin;
To wear to the banquet it never will do,
Then take off the old coat, put on the new,

The new coat is lovely, spotless and pure;
Arrayed in that coat, a welcome is sure;
A place at the feast will be saved for you,
Then take off the old coat, put on the new.

SCRIPTURE READING (GENESIS 3:1–11, 21)

Now the serpent was more crafty than any of the wild animals the Lord God had made. He said to the woman, "Did God really say, 'You must not eat from any tree in the garden'?"

The woman said to the serpent, "We may eat fruit from the trees in the garden, but God did say, 'You must not eat fruit from the tree that is in the middle of the garden, and you must not touch it, or you will die.'"

"You will not certainly die," the serpent said to the woman. "For God knows that when you eat from it your eyes will be opened, and you will be like God, knowing good and evil."

When the woman saw that the fruit of the tree was good for food and pleasing to the eye, and also desirable for gaining wisdom, she took some and ate it. She also gave some to her husband, who was with her, and he ate it. Then the eyes of both of them were opened, and they realized they were naked; so they sewed fig leaves together and made coverings for themselves.

Then the man and his wife heard the sound of the Lord God as he was walking in the garden in the cool of the day, and they hid from the Lord God among the trees of the garden. But the Lord God called to the man, "Where are you?"

He answered, "I heard you in the garden, and I was afraid because I was naked; so I hid."

And he said, "Who told you that you were naked? Have you eaten from the tree that I commanded you not to eat from?"

The Lord God made garments of skin for Adam and his wife and clothed them.

THEOLOGICAL REFLECTION

Italian poet and essayist Giacomo Leopardi's poem "Dialogue Between Fashion and Death" details the connection between death and fashion. The fictional character, Fashion, proclaims to Death, "I am Fashion, your sister." In response to Death's adamant position that there is no kinship between them, Fashion outlines their twin birth. "Do you not remember we are both born of Decay?" While the poem does not fully tell the story of Adam and Eve, even the least religious minds can make the connection.

With an entertaining and amusing flare, the poem outlines the similarities between Fashion and Death, namely that they have no end, and that the pursuit of fashion has led some to extreme discomfort and perhaps even death! The story, as told by Fashion, is so convincing that Death proclaims: "In truth, I believe you are my sister; the testimony of a birth certificate could scarcely make me surer of it." Leopardi wove a colorful picture of Fashion's birth, albeit somewhat inaccurately. For Fashion and Death were not birthed simultaneously in the Garden of Eden: Fashion was birthed before Death and after sin.

In Genesis 3, the Bible recounts the story of clothing's origin. Adam and Eve ate the fruit from the tree of knowledge of good and evil in the center of the Garden of Eden, and in so doing, sinned against God. As a result, for the first time, they saw something other than the beauty and creativity of the human frame; they encountered a sensuality of a different sort, and perhaps, they even became body conscious. A sinking feeling of shame replaced bliss, and the couple did what so many of us do when we sin: they covered themselves and hid from their maker. When Adam and Eve sewed fig leaves together to create aprons to hide their nakedness, the art of fashion was born.

But these fig leaf undergarments were not only inadequate to clothe their bodies; they were also inadequate to cover their guilt and shame. Genesis 3:21 goes on to describe how God stepped in to provide durable clothing for Adam and Eve. This act had profound spiritual implications, as it caused the first animal sacrifice to cover sin, a process that would continue until Jesus Christ came onto the scene. Some theologians posit that the garments were required to make Adam and Eve fit for God's presence.

Thus, because of its aberrant beginning, it is easy to understand why the Christian church has had such an erratic relationship with the art of fashion. Is fashion a frivolous concern of secular society, or does it have a place in God's eternal kingdom? Should modern Christians care about fashion beyond its basic functions of physical protection and moral modesty, or should they denigrate fashion designers as seamstresses of unholy sensuality? Since fashion was born of decay, is it an unredeemable art, or can Jesus's blood redeem it from its original purpose and redesign it into a source and symbol of beauty. Let's take another look at fashion in the biblical narrative!

Be Careful Little Eyes What You See

As Genesis 3 unfolds, Eve found herself alone with Satan, who clothed himself in the scales of a serpent. When Satan questioned her about God's directive regarding the tree of the knowledge of good and evil, and the verity of God's pronouncement that Adam and Eve would die if they touched or ate the fruit, she engaged in a risky conversation. Satan masterfully depicted a different reality, one in which Adam and Eve become like gods. It was the promise of something greater, but little did she know, the promise was an empty lie.

Eve began to question God's instruction and perhaps doubt his intentions. Didn't she and Adam deserve to be like God? Satan was so compelling that Eve adopted the same thinking that caused Satan to be kicked out of heaven (Isa 14:12-14). How dangerous it is to doubt God and twist his word in order to justify our own desires. In Romans 16:17, the apostle Paul warns us to beware those who tell us things contrary to what God has already declared to be true. He tells Timothy that people often seek people who will tell them what they want to hear instead of those who speak the truth (2 Tim 4:3-4).

Why didn't Eve pause to consider what it would mean and be like to know evil? What benefit would it be to know evil—immorality, corruption, depravity? But what was not accomplished with Satan's words, was completed by her eyes as she looked at the fruit of the tree and found it to be pleasant and delightful, harmless even. How strong desire and lust is in the moment that it causes us to flounder and sin at times, and never worry about the consequences until we are faced with them. The desire to be like God and to eat the fruit bred disobedience first in the heart and then in action. Eve ate fruit from the tree and gave it to Adam, who influenced by his wife followed her into folly and disobedience. Then came the realization, as my grandfather used to say, that they had been "duped, hoodwinked, and bamboozled." Their eyes were opened.

Adam and Eve had been physically naked the entire time and felt no shame or discomfort, but sin immediately changed how they saw their nakedness. They no longer felt the innocence, purity, honor, and glory bestowed upon the human frame which God had created in his own image. Their vision of the human body became distorted as it would for every generation to come. The human physique would simultaneously invoke a sense of the aesthetic (good), and provoke lust, vanity, and body consciousness (evil). What's more, we would be birthed into spiritual nudity that needed covering.

Though this couple had long viewed one another openly and freely, they experienced new feelings. They blushed at each other's nakedness and longed to hide from each other and their maker. They creatively covered their flesh with aprons made of fig leaves, birthing fashion into being. This is how it would be for their offspring for all time. We would experience embarrassment from nudity, such that even today most wouldn't dare parade around nude, even in the privacy of their homes. Self-consciousness overcomes us when it comes to our bodies, so we cover them, albeit more fashionably now.

In fact, our clothing is an expression and extension of us. Being clothed makes us feel complete, adequate even as we try to hide or enhance our figures. Our bodies are God's intricate handiwork, but often we see flaws. How sad was the exchange? The loss of freedom, purity and unabashed admiration of beauty replaced by self-doubt and sin.

Garbed in Grace

Garbed in the shame and guilt of sin, Eve and Adam hid from God's presence when they heard his voice. Such is the impact of sin in our lives. It distances us from God and impairs the fellowship we have with him. God called to them, "Where are you?" Adam confessed to hiding so that God could not see their physical nudity, never acknowledging their spiritual nakedness that only God could cover and clothe. The garment of fig leaves that

Adam and Eve created could only hide their physical form that now caused them to blush. Their soul was unclad before the Lord.

God looked upon the fig leaf aprons and saw that they were unfit for the journey that would ensue when the pair would be ousted from the garden. In the face of the elements, their bodies would be at times feeble. The fig aprons were not durable and would not suffice for what was to come. Knowing the experience and life that what awaited the couple, God would ensure that they were adequately clothed physically and spiritually. He demonstrated love, compassion and grace even though Adam and Eve did not deserve it. His showpieces could no longer be on display as intended. God removed the inadequate aprons and exchanged them for something appropriate and lasting. He took life and skin from one of his marvelously crafted creations to cover the beautiful and wonderfully sculpted bodies of the first man and woman. Hence Leopardi's tale of the twin birth of fashion and death.

This first act of sacrificing a life for a life would be repeated throughout Old Testament times. Until Jesus died for our sins, the descendants of Adam and Eve were required to shed the life of an animal, another of God's creations, to get atonement for sins and to cover their spiritual nakedness. It also changed the course of man's interaction with all creation as we would need and use it to cover our bodies. Where Adam and Eve brought death and spiritual destruction into the world, redemption and reconnection to God came through the death of one.

Jesus's death was the ultimate sacrifice after which no other would be required. However, the necessity of clothing would be lasting, and out of that necessity, fashion came to be. Through God's abundant mercy, fashion would become a tool for man to glorify and worship God as we put the work the creativity and skill that God inspired and bestowed. Through fashion, we too would create and design as our Father did.

Fashion in Perspective

Throughout the Bible, we find that fashion served many purposes. In Genesis, Jacob made an ornate robe for his then youngest son, Joseph, to demonstrate the deep love and favor for this child. Fashion was a way to bestow and signal honor, which continues today in many cultures. Unfortunately, it also became a way to distinguish between the classes of people as the rich were able to afford more extravagant clothing and jewelry while the poor could not afford these things.

God also used and reclaimed fashion to distinguish his people from the heathens. In fact, he commissioned skilled workers to design and create garments for Aaron and his sons who were chosen to serve as priests. In Exodus 28:32, God declared that the priestly attire was to be worn, and this would become a lasting ordinance for Aaron and his descendants. It's no wonder so many churches continue the tradition of having pastors, seen as part of the spiritual Aaronic legacy, adorned with ornate robes as they conduct services. However, a growing number of pastors are abandoning this in an effort to be more relatable to the younger generations that have abandoned notions of business and business casual. For what good is the focus on the outer wear, when the inward man is unclean? Or how do we welcome all to worship with us, when our attire draws attention to the wrong things? We will see that this was, in fact, spurred by Jesus's arrival on the scene and his approach to ministering.

In Deuteronomy 22:5, God differentiates between fashion for men and women, disallowing each sex from wearing clothing designed and intended for the opposite sex. God considered this detestable. This had lasting impact secularly and within the church, as it wasn't until the mid-nineteenth century that Western society began to significantly shift its views on women's fashion as the dress reform movement was underway. The middle of the twentieth century marked a global shift in women's clothing and fashion taking on a masculine flair, particularly with the wearing of pants. In many churches, a woman was not permitted to attend, and certainly not serve in any capacity unless "appropriately" clothed in women's attire. For all work and service in the church is done in service to God and is a form of worship and reverence.

Today, the matter of appropriate attire for women in the church differs from denomination to denomination and perhaps even across churches within the same denomination. This is true of the churchgoer's attire overall. There was a time that people sought to wear their "Sunday's best." Christians wore their best clothing as a way of tithing and worshipping even with their attire. By wearing their best clothes and jewelry, and looking their best, they were making a statement of honor and reverence for God. They were giving back the best to the one who provided it in the first place. What a wonderful way to show God gratitude. Imagine that you were invited to meet Queen Elizabeth or some other person of royalty. Would you wear jeans or formal attire to impress? Many would lean towards the latter. This is the notion that drives some churches goers today to dress in their most impressive attire. When they enter the sanctuary, they do so with regard for the Eternal King, who the prophet Isaiah described as "high and exalted, seated on a throne."

Yet many others believe that our fashion should demonstrate the humility and modesty that God requires of the Christian and should not be ornate at all. God attributes far less importance to fashion and our outer appearance than cleanliness of the heart. These believers what place then does fashion have in Christian worship and service? The prophet Isaiah's words were an indication of this shift as it relates to fashion and the church. "I delight greatly in the Lord; my soul rejoices in my God. For he has clothed me with garments of salvation and arrayed me in a robe of his righteousness." (Isa. 61:10) As the ultimate high priest, Jesus gave little heed to the ceremonial laws surrounding a priest's attire. In fact, he instructed his disciples not to worry about materialistic things including our attire. Rather, they needed to attend to their spiritual condition, and as Apostle Paul wrote, be clothed in Christ (Gal 3:27).

Jesus taught in the most unusual of places and this required a level of physical comfort in clothing worn. AsPeople followed him from city to city, they did not wear the most fashionable clothing. This is a statement about how we best worship God through fashion. While identifying as a Christian meant that one's attire would honor Christ, it did not mean that one's fashion and style had to be decorative and high end. In fact, the New Testament writes encouraged the Christian to ensure that their wardrobe was respectful, modest, neat, clean, and appropriately covered the body so as not to cause shame or blushing or invoke lust. The latter was an instruction particularly given to women.

With Jesus and the coming of grace, many of the Jewish spiritual traditions were put aside and the apostles reinforced this. The men were no longer required to wear a turban or head covering. The traditional wearing of a head covering for Jewish men symbolized their shamefacedness and unworthiness to approach the holiest of holies. The Christian was free to approach the throne of grace boldly and look to the father for he was not a servant, but a son. What's more, in some of the pagan cultures of that day, men wore head coverings to pray to their gods. Removing this requirement shifted how men engaged in worship.

Women, however, were expected to wear a head covering in public worship because the man was the head, and she was subject to him. A covering symbolized modesty, chastity, as well as subordination and honor for her husband. Not only did women have to cover her head in worship, but engaging in hair fashions that resulted in the cutting of a woman's hair was the equivalent of not wearing a head covering. A woman's hair was an adornment and part of her beauty. The fashion of wearing a head covering meant subjection for the female, while not wearing one was a sign of spiritual liberty for the male.

Today, many Christians question these expectations, while some churches still prescribe gender distinctions to worship Christ. This is true of many Apostolic and a few Pentecostal churches. There is a beauty that women have naturally that can be enhanced by fashion in a way that is not true for men. This is what gives rise to a whole industry geared towards females.

For modern believers, fashion is a matter of the heart—something that is between them and God. Of course, it is influenced by the culture and the church that one attends, but at the heart of the matter is how we individually honor God and give him our best through our fashion style. This is a matter of means and intention and one that we each must grapple with on our own. But it is a wonderful opportunity to praise the Creator with our form and fashion. We are free in Christ and not bound to the customs of men.

Our fashion should reflect the honor due to God in the way that we are led to express it. It is equally acceptable to dress up to bring and be your best before God, and to dress modestly in respect and regard for him. Both have the same intention. Fashion is a form of worship as it is one of the few ways we are able to visually express our individuality and culture and show the creativity that God has fostered in us. We must do so in a way that brings honor, not embarrassment.

For those in the industry, fashion design is a calling. Just as God worked during creation, they work and create using the gift provided by the Creator. They play a deeper role still as they influence the fashion trends of the broader culture, which inevitably reaches our churches. Christians in fashion have a responsibility to help shape the trends in a way that honors God. God redeemed fashion for his use and for our benefit. It is unique in that we become the visual art form as we adorn, accentuate, and beautify our outer appearance and in so do honor the gift of creativity that God gave us.

Conclusion

While fashion is ever-changing, it always seems to return to days gone by and is often dictated by the culture of the day. There is an expectation that God has of believers to pursue fashion in a way that honors him, and our bodies. We are not to simply adopt the fashion cues of the day, but to combat them when ill contrived. We are to be in the world, but not of it. We are to be a light, and we can do so with our physical and spiritual attire. In our own way, we must ensure that we are adequately clothed.

PRAYER

Father, I am grateful for the gift of self-expression, creativity, and beauty that you have given through fashion. Guide us as we seek to honor you with our attire and style. Help us to uphold the expectations and restrictions you have wisely put in place. Though we have freedom, help us to ensure that our outer appearance is not a distraction or stumbling block for those who seek to see and understand you. May my fashion and style reflect my culture and personality, and let your creativity and temperance prevail in me. May my inward heart and my outward appearance glorify you. In Jesus's name. Amen.

DISCUSSION QUESTIONS

1. If our fashion is a way to worship God, does your style communicate what you want?
2. The New Testament provides some expectations for Christian male and female fashion. What does it look like for you individually? As a church community?
3. Today's fashion and style are driven by a highly sexualized culture. How then do we redeem fashion for ourselves?
4. We have freedom of self-expression in fashion that allows us to communicate who we are including reflecting our generational voice and culture. In fact, many people look at us and size us up based on our fashion. How is Christ then represented in this freedom and in your own sense of fashion?
5. Some would say that there are clear gender differences in terms of the significance and power of fashion even in the church, tipping in favor of women. Do you think that fashion is more powerful for one sex over the other in the church?

SPIRITUAL EXERCISES

1. Considering that your personal style glorifies God as the creative freedom he has given us is reflected in your church wear. Consider what you want to communicate to God through your style. As you prepare for each service, put together an outfit that beautifully tells God all that you hope to say.

2. As a church community host a bible study series on the intersection of fashion, faith, and worship. Walk through the history of fashion in the Bible from Genesis through the New Testament. Does the church have a culture as it relates to fashion and if so what is the spiritual significance of this? Culminate with a worship through fashion week or month where members are encouraged to express their adoration and reverence for God in their Sunday style. Encourage members to share their appreciation for each other's choices for worship through style and fashion.

3. Also, if there are local fashion designers of faith, schedule a talk and ask them to share how they approach their design process, how they worship God through their personal style, and some of their designs and the character and beauty they see in them. Pray for them and their influence locally, regionally, and nationally. If members are interested, pay a visit to a store that sells their designs to look at the beauty created by their hands, pray for their success, and consider making a purchase.

RESOURCES FOR FURTHER REFLECTION

1. *J's Everyday Fashion and Faith: Personal Style with Purpose* by Jeanette Johnson
2. *Modest Fashion: Styling Bodies, Mediating Faith* edited by Reina Lewis
3. *A Tailored Fit Life: Faith and Fashion Guide* by Samantha Murray
4. "Made Well: A Glimpse at the Theology of Fashion," https://thepoint-magazine.org/988/stories/made-well-a-glimpse-at-the-theology-of-fashion/
5. *Fashion, Faith and Following Jesus,* https://churchleaders.com/worship/worship-articles/162935-fashion-faith-and-following-jesus.html
6. *Fashion Meets Faith,* online style community, https://fashionmeetsfaith.com/about/
7. *My Chic Obsession,* https://www.mychicobsession.com/can-fashion-glorify-god-other-thoughts-about-god-and-work/
8. *A Pocketful of Faith: A Faith, Fashion and Life Blog,* https://apocketfulloffaith.com/

Chapter 5

The Dance of Redemption
The Art of Ballet

Jonathan Romig

Four Dancers (c.1899) by Edgar Degas

The French artist Edgar Degas (1834–1917) was born in Paris where he would spend much of his life painting, sculpting, and creating works of art, often capturing artists making art. He is most famous for painting ballet dancers behind the scenes, in class or rehearsing a performance. He used pastels and oils, fluctuating somewhere between impressionism and realism, to capture the movement, delicacy, and complexity of ballet like none other has. As Degas observed art in the making, and let it move him to create his own works, we too can be inspired by his artistry to create something beautiful of our own.

Degas painted the *Four Dancers* (c. 1899) by photographing a female dancer. He adapted the oranges and greens in the negative to create this scene of four ballerinas dancing on a stage against a pastoral backdrop. His use of light and dark provide contrast and shape. While the ballet dancers prepare to perform, we too prepare to receive the gift of ballet and what it might have to tell us about God and his beauty. We let Degas and his dancers take us not by the hand but by the heart, drawing us in, preparing us to leap and dance among fields of green.

CALL TO WORSHIP (PSALM 30:4–5, 11–12)

Leader: Sing the praises of the Lord, you his faithful people; praise his holy name.

People: For his anger lasts only a moment, but his favor lasts a lifetime, weeping may stay for the night, but rejoicing comes in the morning.

Leader: You turned my wailing into dancing; you removed my sackcloth and clothed me with joy, that my heart may sing your praises and not be silent.

People: Lord my God, I will praise you forever.

SONG "SIMPLE GIFTS"—SHAKER SONG (1848)

'Tis the gift to be simple, 'tis the gift to be free
'Tis the gift to come down where we ought to be,
And when we find ourselves in the place just right,
'Twill be in the valley of love and delight.

When true simplicity is gained,
To bow and to bend we shan't be ashamed,
To turn, turn will be our delight,
Till by turning, turning we come 'round right.

POEM "THEY WHO DANCE" BY MARJORIE ALLEN SEIFFERT (1920)

The feet of dancers
Shine with mirth,
Their hearts are vibrant as bells:
The air flows by them
Divided like water
Cut by a gleaming ship.
Triumphantly their bodies sing,
Their eyes are blind
With music.
They move through threatening ghosts
Feeling them cool as mist
On their brows.
They who dance
Find infinite golden floors
Beneath their feet.

SCRIPTURE READING (SONGS OF SONGS 2:8–10)

The voice of my beloved!
    Behold, he comes,
      leaping over the mountains,
        bounding over the hills.
My beloved is like a gazelle
    or a young stag.
Behold, there he stands
    behind our wall,
gazing through the windows,
    looking through the lattice.
My beloved speaks and says to me:
"Arise, my love, my beautiful one,
    and come away,

THEOLOGICAL REFLECTION

The ballet *Giselle* is a love story between a young frail maiden named Giselle and a nobleman, Count Albrecht. Giselle lives in a small village with her mother where the villagers are preparing to celebrate the Wine Festival. The local huntsman Hilarion loves Giselle but hides his feelings. Count Albrecht comes to the village disguised as a peasant. He too has fallen in love with Giselle and is determined to win her affection. They flirt and dance, but the Hilarion breaks up their romance. Hilarion grows suspicious that this peasant is more than he seems.

When the villagers return from harvesting grapes, they all begin to dance, but Giselle's mother warns that she is too frail for love. If she dies of a broken heart, in death she will be transformed into a "wilis," a restless and vengeful spirit that haunts men caught in the forest late at night.

When a prince and his daughter join the party, Count Albrecht slips away so as not to be discovered. However, the princess discovers both she and Giselle are engaged, and she gifts Giselle with a beautiful necklace. The celebration is soon ruined when Hilarion, having discovered Albrecht's secret, exposes him for an imposter. He is not a peasant but a Count, and it turns out, is engaged to the prince's daughter, the one who gave Giselle the necklace.

Giselle is devastated. She loved the man she thought was a peasant but turns out to be a deceitful nobleman. Her frail mind crumbles and she dies, her heart in pieces. Act I of the ballet *Giselle* ends in brokenness, despair, and death. The dance has come to an end, and it has not ended in joy.

The ballet *Giselle* shares many themes with the scriptures: love, passion, conflict, joy, betrayal, death, hope. *Giselle* helps us draw these themes out as we think of the Bible and its stories as one extended dance, one long story. The metaphor of dance helps us capture and express some of the feelings and emotions we encounter in Scripture. While words sometimes fall short, dance helps us soar, drawing our hearts upward in worship. The Bible's dance, like every ballet, begins with a single step.

The first step of the Bible's dance is in the first book, Genesis chapter one. Creation bursts forth like a cosmic dance as the Spirit of God soars over the waters (Gen 1:1). God beckons the world and beauty into being. He places the very best of humankind, Adam and Eve, in a garden to keep it. They are called to the dance floor and all of creation is watching. Adam and Eve dance with each other and with God, the three in perfect harmony, but it will not last.

A serpent slithers his way across the garden. He tempts Adam and Eve to dance no longer with God but with him alone. They and all humanity take the bait. We bite the fruit but the taste is bitter. We transform from perfection and harmony in communion with God to a stumbling, warped, and broken mess. We break the dance by dancing with the devil instead of our Creator. Like a leaping dancer who tears a tendon, we fall.

The question then, is what will happen in Act II? Will we, like Giselle and Count Albrecht, dance again? Does God invite us to the dance anew? Will he give us another shot? Though we fell, our God never stopped dancing, never stopped the story of creation. Now he invites us to come and dance the dance of redemption with him.

Our redeemer invites us to come and dance. Our Creator invites us, yes beckons us, to come and enter into relationship with him. Our relationship with God is like a dance. Will we let him lead us or will we dance to our own tune? To dance alone is to dance with the serpent in the dirt.

God is not content to leave us on our own. Like a groom loves his bride, God is bound and determined to dance with his loved ones again. We find the picture of marriage in the scriptures that echoes that greater love story between God and humankind.

We find God's greater dance in human hearts in the Song of Songs, a romantic love song between a bride and groom, a husband and wife. Together they discover the rhythm and beauty of love and marriage, and so teach us about God's love for his beloved people. See how the groom comes leaping for his bride, eager and ready to know her. That's how God desires us.

See how the bride exults in her groom's adoration? She hears his voice and rejoices. See how she anticipates his joy and admires his strength? See how he both affirms her yet calls her into deeper relationship? Together they find a special and beautiful marriage only they share. And yet their marriage, their deep connection, is but a blurry image of a much greater reality.

In the Old Testament God describes his relationship with Israel as one of marriage. Though Israel resists and dances with other partners, her husband extends his hand again and again (Jer 31:32–33). In the New Testament, human marriage is but a dance rehearsal of a much greater performance, Christ's love for the gathering of believers he calls church and bride (Eph 5:25).

Human marriage is like a black and white photo of the Sistine chapel, God's relationship with his people, Christ's relationship with the church. That is the true beauty human marriage pictures. But we resist our groom. My heart grows cold. Despite having the best dance partner in the universe, we still want to lead at cost to our own beauty. I would rather dance by myself than with him, the perfect dance partner.

A ballerina can perform great feats alone. She is elegant and beautiful. Yet a man and a woman can perform even greater feats together. Author Gary Thomas writes of ballet dancing in his book *Cherish*:

Famed Russian-born ballet choreographer George Balanchine once said, "Ballet is woman." The best male dancers recognize that their role is all about showcasing the female dancer's beauty, particularly during pas de deux—couples' dancing. People generally go to the ballet to see the beautiful form, grace, balance, coordination, and strength of the female lead, but all of those qualities are even better showcased when the ballerina has a male dancer who can set her up, catch her, and support her.[1]

As a former male dancer and later choreographer, Balanchine said his job was to "make the beautiful more beautiful." God made us beautiful. Even in the darkness of the fall humans still shine with his glory; but oh, how we could shine so much more brightly if we danced with him. Couples's dance is like our relationship with God. Apart from him we can create beauty, but when we accept his invitation to dance, our lives become an eternal work of art. Our redeemer invites us to come and dance. Will you accept the invitation? Will you take his hand? He wants to redeem us. That means he wants to restore our relationship with God to be even better than the garden. Will you let him dance the dance of redemption with you?

Maybe you're not ready. You're asking, "What type of dance is this? Will this dance be happy or sad, easy or hard? Are we dancing the tango, swing, hip-hop, blues, or ballet?" We're all asking the same questions, "What is relationship with God like? How will the story go?" Classical ballet is a distinct yet precise, light yet graceful, form of dance. They call ballet, "poetry in motion." Likewise, our relationship with God is something distinct, something different, something poetic. If we look at the greater-dance, the story of redemption throughout the Bible, we find God's relationship with us is three things.

First, the dance of redemption is tragic yet joyful. It breaks our hearts and restores our spirits. Second, the dance of redemption humbles yet exalts. It brings us low only to lift us up. Third, the dance of redemption wounds yet redeems. It breaks us and remakes us.

The Dance of Redemption is Tragic Yet Joyful

Our relationship with God is bitter yet sweet. In the Old Testament the women would dance for the men as they came home from victory in battle (Judg 11:34; Song 6:13; Jer 31:4). I imagine that even as they danced some were weeping. The dance God dances with us often starts with sorrow before

---

1. Thomas, *Cherish*, 43.

turning to joy. Ecclesiastes 3:1,4 tells us there is a time for sadness and a time for happiness and dance.

> For everything there is a season,
> and a time for every matter under heaven:
> a time to weep, and a time to laugh;
> a time to mourn, and a time to dance;

Dance in the Old Testament is often the cure for sadness. The psalmist David, the greatest King of Israel, wrote a song of celebration for the dedication of the temple, a bitter-sweet event he never saw in his lifetime. In Psalm 30:11 David envisioned it to be an incredibly joyful event full of dancing even though he would not be there.

> You have turned for me my mourning into dancing;
> you have loosed my sackcloth
> and clothed me with gladness,

Dance is a way to express joy. Dancing is both a result of joy and can produce joy. It's a way we can thank God for turning our sorrow into something valuable. When we dance this way, we're echoing that greater dance of our Creator come to rescue us, the dance of redemption.

When God led Israel out of captivity in Egypt the people celebrated the first Passover, a meal meant to remind them of their deliverance from bondage. The original languages tell us "the Hebrew verb *pāsach* . . . 'to perform a limping dance,' is the root of 'Pesach' or Passover."[2] When Israel left captivity in Egypt, there must have been dancing, but dancing with a limp. Joy is born out of hurt. We limp when God takes those we love but our hearts dance because we know they are with him. We limp when hard things happen and God offers no answer but we dance because God is still good. We limp today but we will dance tomorrow because Jesus loves us forever. "You have turned for me my mourning into dancing."

After Passover, God rescued his people from the hand of Pharaoh at the crossing of the Red Sea. When Pharaoh's armies were about to destroy them, God brought the waves crashing down upon them. As the people stood on the far shore, Moses's sister Miriam broke into a dance of praise (Ps 150:4). She and the women danced not for any man's victory, but for God's victory over Pharaoh and his armies.

---

2 Ackerman, "Dance," 311.

> Then Miriam the prophetess, the sister of Aaron, took a tambourine in her hand, and all the women went out after her with tambourines and dancing. And Miriam sang to them:
> "Sing to the Lord, for he has triumphed gloriously;
> the horse and his rider he has thrown into the sea." (Exod 15:20–2)

We praise God when our dance with him is easy and when it is hard, when life makes sense and when it stings. Ballets like *Swan Lake* and *Romeo and Juliet* express emotions both happy and sad in ways our words fail. It is no wonder that so many Bible stories are told in ballets: Jean Börlin's *La Creation du Monde*, George Balanchine's *Noah and the Flood* and *The Prodigal Son*, Vaslav Nijinsky's *The Legend of Joseph*, Ninette de Valois's *Job*, Martha Graham's *Hérodiade*, and Kenneth MacMillan's *The Judas Tree*. All the Bible's stories with their great leaps and deep falls are telling a greater story, one of redemption. Our redeemer invites us to come and dance the dance of redemption, which is tragic yet joyful.

The Dance of Redemption Humbles Yet Exalts

In our dance with God, he humbles us before exalting us. He dips us low before lifting us high. Throughout the Bible he humbles those he loves time and time again before raising them up to new heights. One of those he especially loved, was King David, a man after his own heart. When David was king over Israel, he decided to bring the Ark of the Covenant to Jerusalem. The ark was a golden chest where God's presence resided. As David was leading the processional into the city of Jerusalem, he danced and leaped, flinging his whole self before the Lord. The picture must have been a wild scene because not everyone was impressed, including his wife.

> And David danced before the Lord with all his might. . . As the ark of the Lord came into the city of David, Michal the daughter of Saul looked out of the window and saw King David leaping and dancing before the Lord, and she despised him in her heart. . . And David said to Michal, ". . .I will celebrate before the Lord. 22 I will make myself yet more contemptible than this, and I will be abased in your eyes. (2 Sam 6:14a, 16, 21–22a)

David humbled himself before the Lord through dance. There is something deeply humbling about dance. There is a loss of dignity for the sake of beauty. The professional ballerina Corina Gill says, "Vulnerability and suffering goes into art." It is that vulnerability and suffering that creates beauty.

David puts all he has into his offering of worship before the Lord. He makes much of God by making little of himself. We too enter into the dance of redemption by humbling ourselves, worshipping him at cost to our own pride. We lay our whole life before him and when he so desires, he will lift us up. He will lift us up higher than we can ever imagine.

Ezekiel 28 tells us the Garden of Eden was on a mountaintop (Gen. 2:10; Ezek 28:13-14). Isaiah 6 tells us that one day God is going to again establish his eternal city on a mountaintop where heaven and earth meet (Isa 2:1-4; Rev 21:1-4). All throughout Scripture we find brief glimpses of what that eternal mountaintop relationship will be like. In the Song of Songs 2:8 the beloved "comes, leaping over the mountains, bounding over the hills." (Song 8:14) In the face of intense hardships and despair, the prophet Habakkuk says of his relationship with God:

> God, the Lord, is my strength;
> he makes my feet like the deer's;
> he makes me tread on my high places. (Hab 3:19)

If you are in a valley with your walk with God, God seems distant and far, he will not always leave you there. If you are on a mountaintop with your walk with God, enjoy the view, maybe dance a little because God has put you there, at least for a season. One day God will lift all who trust him up to the highest peaks to dance like a deer on the high places forever and ever. Our redeemer invites us to come and dance. The dance of redemption is tragic yet joyful, humbles yet exalts, and . . .

The Dance of Redemption Wounds Yet Redeems

If we try to dance through this life without God, we will find we always fall short of his glory (Rom 3:23). We try to be good and kind, and much of the time we are, but like someone with two left feet, we often trip over ourselves and those we love. We sin and our sin wounds us deep inside. Often, our sin wounds others too. We need a someone to lead us in a better dance.

The ballerina Corina Gill says she has seen a tiny dancer fill the stage by just standing there. We too have a master dancer, God himself, who has stepped out onto the stage and into the spotlight. Our redeemer has come in the silhouette of God's one and only Son, the greatest glory in a frail human body.

As the spotlight shines on the Son it finds him spotless in every way. His pose is regal, his head held high. He truly fills the stage. All eyes are on him as he dances. He leaps and soars, strong and sure. His life is sinless, perfect. Another figure enters the stage. This one is all dressed in black, one seen in the world's brokenness yet unseen in the world's eyes. The devil rages and roars. Jesus dances on, never missing a beat, always holy, always good. His dance takes him to the cross where he puts all his vulnerability and suffering into his art. He sacrifices himself unto death so that we might join him in life. By his wounds we are healed (Isa. 53:5). The gospel of John tells us of his redemptive dance.

> "For God so loved the world, that he gave his only Son, that whoever believes in him should not perish but have eternal life. (John 3:16)

Jesus redeems our darkness, our scars, our sins, so that we might step into the spotlight spotless. The devil has nothing on us now. The curtain of death closes on the principal dancer but for a moment, three days. When the tomb opens again, he is somehow even more glorious than before. He shines with the brightest love, the strongest strength, the oldest power.

Will you recognize him for who he is? So many have missed him (Matt 11:17). Will you dance? Will you accept Christ's hand? If your heart is wounded with your sin, come and dance with Jesus. Come and enter into relationship with him. He is our principal dancer, our hero, our king. He can forgive you and remake you. Come and dance with him.

Conclusion

The dance of redemption is tragic yet joyful, humbles yet exalts, wounds yet redeems. Our redeemer invites us to come and dance. Will you take his hand? This invitation takes us back to the ballet, *Giselle*. In Act II, Giselle is dead. The huntsman Hilarion comes to her tombstone late at night, grief-stricken and guilty. Out of the woods the wilis come, the spirits of wronged maidens who died with unfulfilled love beating in their hearts. For his sins the queen of the wilis sentences Hilarion to dance until he dies. Exhausted, he perishes.

Then Count Albrecht comes to Giselle's tombstone, dismayed and sorrowful. His love led to her death. Out of the grave Giselle's spirit rises as a wilis, but so too, the queen of the wilis comes with her vengeful spirits all dressed in white, brides of death. The queen captures Albrecht. Although Giselle begs for mercy, stretching wide her arms to protect him, the queen condemns him to dance until he dies; but Albrecht does not dance alone. Giselle dances with him.

Giselle, the frail of heart, rescues Albrecht by dancing with him through the night. When he collapses and cannot dance any longer, when death is near, she raises him up, higher together than he ever could have danced alone. Together they dance until the morning rises, breaking the queen's curse. Giselle descends back into her grave and Albrecht, for a moment lays his hands on her tombstone, the shape of the cross.

Giselle is the Christ figure. She is the innocent maiden. She perishes because of the sin of others. And yet, even in death she grants life. When Albrecht is condemned, she saves him, and suffers with him, bringing him through the dark valley of death. This is what Jesus did for us. He gave his life so that we might live, and he is still giving his life today so that any who trust him with their lives will continue dancing, even in the dark. The sun will come again, morning will come, but still he remains. Our redeemer invites us to come and dance. Will you take his hand?

PRAYER

Heavenly Father, thank you for the Spirit's cosmic flight over the watery chaos of creation. You called us into being to dance the dance of relationship with you. We stumbled and fell in Adam and Eve. We sinned and turned away, determined to dance alone to our own destruction. The world's dance was not as it should be. So much brokenness and shame, even in me.

Thank you for sending your Son, Christ Jesus, to dance the dance of redemption. Thank you that he will make us his bride, his dancing partner for all eternity. We look in hope for that coming day when our Redeemer will come leaping and bounding over the mountains and hills. He will come and lead us into forever joy. Prepare our hearts for his. May he lead us every day. We praise you Father for your Son. In Jesus name, amen.

DISCUSSION QUESTIONS

1. What is your favorite type of dance? Why?
2. How does dance illustrate our relationship with God?
3. What Scripture passage on dance resonates with you the most? Why?
4. Why can dance feel so embarrassing? What can this teach us about worship?
5. What do you think of the vision of a redeemer God inviting you to dance? What's keeping you back from dancing with Jesus?

SPIRITUAL EXERCISES

1. Attend ballet with a friend or group of friends from your church. Reflect on the theological themes you find in the music, choreography, and storyline. What does it tell you about God and yourself?

2. Watch a performance of *Giselle* or another ballet on YouTube or Amazon Prime. Reflect on it afterwards. I recommend the one-hour, fifty-minute, 2006 version: *Giselle*—Laëticia Pujol, Nicolas Le Riche—Opéra National de Paris.

3. Take thirty minutes to journal about your life story. How has God been dancing with you through the years? Have you noticed him before? What are you noticing now? How has he led you and how would you like him to lead you going forward?

4. Find a private space all by yourself, play a favorite hymn, praise music, or modern song, then dance. Dance with all of your might. No one will know but you and your King.

5. Sign up for a dance class. Ask the teacher how their dance connects to their spirituality. What similarities do you see with your own faith? What differences?

6. Purchase a painting, photograph, or print of ballet or your favorite type of dance. Put it somewhere you will enjoy it. Every time you see it remember the dance of redemption and how Christ is reaching out to dance with you.

RESOURCES FOR FURTHER REFLECTION

1. *Ballet: The Definitive Illustrated Story* by DK and Viviana Durante
2. *Dancing Through It: My Journey in the Ballet* by Jenifer Ringer.
3. *It Was Good: Performing Arts to the Glory of God* by Ned Bustard.
4. *The Art of Movement* by Ken Browar and Deborah Ory

Chapter 6

Losing Sight of the Choreographer

The Art of Choreography

TRIP WEILER

El Jaleo (1882) by John Singer Sargent

American expatriate painter John Singer Sargent (1856–1925) was born in Florence to American parents and trained as a painter in Paris before moving to London. Considered one of the greatest landscape artists of his time, he also achieved international acclaim as a portrait painter. Prolific throughout his career, he created over nine hundred oil paintings, two thousand watercolors, and countless sketches and charcoal drawings. Many of his paintings were inspired by his extensive travels throughout America, Europe, and the Middle East.

Sargent's massive painting *El Jaleo* currently hangs in the Isabella Stewart Gardener Museum in Boston. It is based on drawings he made during a trip to southern Spain in 1879. The name *El Jaleo* is roughly translated "a ruckus" and refers to an Andalusian dance known as *jaleo de jerez*. Sargent's dramatized contrast between deep blacks and the shining white skirt of the dancer creates a sense of movement where the observer can almost hear the sounds of singing and guitars and feel the heels clicking and hands clapping among the festive throng.

CALL TO WORSHIP (ADAPTED FROM UNITING CHURCH IN AUSTRALIA, SYNOD OF VICTORIA AND TASMANIA)

Leader: Father God, who taught the earth to dance silently through space:

People: We celebrate your beauty and your grace.

Leader: Planet earth, gleaming green and blue, Your Creator commands:

People: "Rejoice in your ocean currents, as they dance and swirl with hope."

Leader: Planet earth, pulsing with life, join with the angels in the Divine Dance:

People: With all your flora and fauna, dance and sing praises to the Lord.

Leader: Planet earth, enveloped in the breath of God:

People: May God bless all your creatures this day, with His life-giving breath.

Leader: We thank You, Divine Dancer, our Creator, for planet earth, our precious, fragile home:

People: Celebrate and dance, all children, creatures, and all created things.

Leader: O earth, O people, and all created things, dance in God's presence!

People: Spin and dance, planet earth, spin and dance for God!

Leader: We celebrate the dance of our planet!

People: Sing, earth, sing and dance! For our God is the Lord of the Dance!

HYMN "PRAISE YE THE LORD, LET PRAISE EMPLOY" BY ANNE STEELE (1769)

Praise ye the Lord, let praise employ
In His own courts, your songs of joy;
The spacious firmament around
Shall echo back the joyful sound.

Recount His works in strains divine,
His wondrous works, how bright they shine!
Praise Him for all His mighty deeds,
Whose greatness all your praise exceeds.

Awake the trumpet's piercing sound,
To spread your sacred pleasure round;
While softer music tunes the lute,
The warbling harp, the breathing flute.

Ye virgin train, with joy advance,
To praise Him in the graceful dance;
Awake each voice and strike each string,
And to the solemn organ sing.

Let cymbals loud now sound on high
To softer, deeper notes reply;
armonious let the concert rise,
And bear the rapture to the skies.

Let all whom life and breath inspire
Attend and join the blissful choir;
But chiefly ye who know His Word,
Adore and love and praise the Lord.

SCRIPTURE READING (MATTHEW 22:34–40)

Now when the Pharisees heard that he had silenced the Sadducees, they assembled together. And one of them, an expert in religious law, asked him a question to test him: 'Teacher, which commandment in the law is the greatest?' Jesus said to him, "'Love the Lord your God with all your heart, with all your soul, and with all your mind.' This is the first and greatest commandment. The second is like it: 'Love your neighbor as yourself.' All the law and the prophets depend on these two commandments.

THEOLOGICAL REFLECTION

I'll never forget our first Christmas after moving to the Berkshire Mountains in western Massachusetts. I was only six months into my first senior pastorate—talk about getting your sea legs underneath you. And both of my daughters had fallen in love with dance, ballet in particular. This brought tremendous joy to my wife. She would say, "Ballet is my first love, after Jesus!" "What about your husband?" someone might ask. But I learned a long time ago that some questions are better left unanswered. My wife is a beautiful dancer and a masterful choreographer.

So, finding a new dance studio for our daughters was of utmost importance. At the girls' previous dance studio back in Maryland, it became a tradition in the Weiler family for our girls to dance in the production of *The Nutcracker* during Christmastide. Thankfully, the new studio checked all boxes, and it even offered the opportunity for the girls to continue the tradition of dancing in *The Nutcracker*. That year my oldest daughter was cast as a toy soldier, and my youngest was to be an angel. Cue the collective "Aaaawwww!"

Understandably, my wife was eager to get involved with the production: helping with costumes, running numbers with children who couldn't remember the choreography, and even just wrangling the young'uns when they weren't rehearsing.

Everyone was excited for the week of the production, but during the first rehearsal with costumes, the director/choreographer kept rhythmically slapping her hands together and shouting, "I know you're happy to be in your costumes, but you need to focus! We have a show to do in three nights! Yes, the costumes are wonderful, but they won't mean anything if you don't know the dance!" A slap accompanied each enunciated word.

It was finally the moment my youngest was waiting for: the opening of Act II—The Magic Castle—when the angels actually get to dance with the

Sugar Plum Fairy. In their sparkly tutus and flittering wings that bounced with every motion, a dozen six and seven-year-olds couldn't contain their excitement any longer. Giggling, some screeching with joy and laughter, spinning with their wiggling wings, and bouncing all over the stage, they spun and jiggled right into the Sugar Plum Fairy, Clara and the Nutcracker Prince (all leads, and all somberly intent upon perfecting every step, every breath of motion). Like Mount Vesuvius, the red-faced choreographer erupted, terrifying everyone in the theatre: "No! No! No! Don't ever lose sight of the dance! Angels, do you see what you did? You lost focus and turned beautiful choreography into complete chaos! Angels, go away, take a breath, and start again! Remember the dance!"

Forgetting the Dance

Before I received a vocational calling to be a pastor, my goal was to be a Broadway star. The drama "bug" bit me in the fourth grade. I didn't see myself doing anything other than performing. But even in my earliest productions in elementary school, I was terrified of the choreographer. The choreographer was the only one, it seemed, who could override the director—even interrupt the dress rehearsal! Remembering the choreography seemed to be just as important as remembering our lines and the lyrics to the songs. The choreographer would get so upset when we messed up the dance. But why? What's the big deal? I wanted to ask these questions, but I never had the courage to do it.

But as I gained more experience in theatre, the answers to these questions became clear: forgetting the choreography was disrespectful and insulting, not only to the choreographer and the director, but to everyone else involved with the production. What we did (or didn't do) impacted the entire production. And forgetting the choreography could be dangerous—wrong steps would not only hurt our egos, but they could actually cause a serious injury if we fell into each other. I eventually understood why the choreography was so crucial.

Sometimes I wonder if we, human beings, have forgotten the dance in the production of life. Have we lost sight of the Choreographer? When faced with what seems to be global chaos: whether war, economic upheaval, pandemics, racial injustice, genocide, natural disasters, or even the problem of evil itself, we hear the cries: "Where is God in all this? Why would God allow this? Or even, is God punishing us with this disaster?"

First of all, we must be careful with some of these questions. Yes, of course, God invites us to reason with him, as Isaiah 1:18 encourages. God desires for all of his people to raise tough questions and wrestle with the perplexing problems of life. But we tread on dangerous ground when we assume that all unpleasant circumstances are either a divine cause or consequence for sin. God's punishment for sin. In fact, God admonishes Job for doing this very thing (Job 38).

As God's created beings, who are we to understand the mind of the Creator? It would be like the statue David interrogating Michelangelo, "Why are you putting my hand like this? Why are you chiseling off that bit of marble there? I don't want my toes facing this direction!?" I could imagine Michelangelo's response, much like God's to us, "Quiet! Just trust me and let me work. It's not for you to concern yourself with such things. I know what I'm doing."

Theologian Alister McGrath says:

> There is no way in which a created human being would be capable of beholding God directly. As a result, we need to think of God in a scaled-down manner, appropriate to our ability to cope. Some early Christian writers used to compare understanding God with looking directly into the sun. The human eye is simply not capable of withstanding the full brilliance of the sun. In the same way, the human mind cannot cope with the full glory of God.[1]

Thus ,It would be dangerous for human beings to comprehend the mind of God because it would lead them to undermine his plan, his choreography, as it were, for humanity on earth.

When we read Genesis 1, as God creates the heavens and the earth, he repeatedly and rhythmically says, "Let there be light . . . let there be . . . a vault to separate water from water . . . let there be . . . water gathered in one place . . . let there be . . . land and vegetation" and so on. N.T. Wright calls this a "lavishing 'let there be.'"[2] God is lavishly creating and commissioning.

The phrase "Let there be" means several things at once. Of course, it means "to come into existence," but at the same time, it also means "to endure, to repeat, to remain existing"; there are even elements of "prediction" and "adaptation." Think about the implications for a moment: in creating the universe, God crafted the planets and set the stars alight. He choreographed their movements—their orbits, and the dance of gravity and its effects on surrounding objects, even whole solar systems. The universe is constantly moving, adapting, changing. On earth, mountains rise, snow falls, winds blow, and trees grow.

---

1. McGrath, *Theology*, 23.
2. Wright, *Ask N.T. Wright Anything Podcast*, episode 14.

God also designed the dance cycles of birth and death in his creatures. He choreographed the oceans and their currents, the land and all of its ecosystems, gathered animals travelling in arranged herds, the sky and the movement of airstreams and moisture, the cycles of rain and seasons, and even bacterial and viral systems which, if the earth is stewarded as God intended, are actually healthy for environments, vegetation, and even life itself. God created all of this—he choreographed the movement and momentum of all things, blessed it, and commissioned it to exist, to move, and to dance!

So, when God created human beings, the crown of his creative efforts, the lords and ladies of the dance, as it were, his declaration "it was very good" was both a blessing and a commissioning. When taken all together, the words "dominion," "rule," and "subdue," it's as if he is saying to humanity: "Look, I created everything with momentum, energy, and movement. I created the earth and all of its systems, seen and unseen, for you, my children, to harness with wisdom and humility. Rule over it all, care for all of it, and benefit from all these things, and then share the blessing with your fellow humankind. You are a key partner in the choreography of creation."

But have we succeeded in doing this? Have we, as human beings, worked together to shepherd, steward, and humbly harness the earth and all of its extensive systems? I think not. As with every decision we make, there are physical and spiritual implications. Over the last decade, with the progression of technology and social media, we are more "connected" than ever. But humanity has, perhaps, never been so more divided.

Our communities are alienated, and our common dignity has been stripped bare. Social graces, etiquette, manners, cultural respect, and decorum have been greatly diminished. We've lost our sense of civility and have become selfish, segregated, and aggressively reactive. We've pushed God out of the dance altogether. We've now forgotten the choreography in virtually every sphere of the dance. And we've insisted on following our own steps, we've slammed the door in the face of the Choreographer and fallen into chaos.

God choreographed the perfect production for us to thrive and flourish, but our missteps allowed sin to cut into God's dance, thus disrupting and distracting us from God's intended choreography. As a result, we have lost sight of the choreographer and have forgotten the dance.

A Divine Dance Partner

So, has the dance come to an end? Has he abandoned the people he created? Has God found a different dance partner in another universe? Absolutely not! God is sovereign over every aspect of his creation, even sin. He is still there.

As a matter of fact, after humanity fell out of step and forgot the dance, God choreographed a new dance; a beautiful dance of redemption to restore the broken production. He sent his own son, Jesus Christ, to dance on centerstage. Jesus danced at the wedding in Cana, where he revealed his divine nature by turning water into wine. He danced when he healed the blind, deaf, and lame. He danced when he raised his friend Lazarus from the dead. He danced as he caried his cross all the way up the hill to Golgotha. And he danced over the tomb of sin and death when he was resurrected on the third day.

And with resurrected legs and new life, he invites all of humanity to join him in the dance. As our divine dance partner, he has extended an open invitation for us to follow him in the dance of forgiveness and restoration. The cosmic Choreographer is still designing; he is still dancing; he still wants us to join him in the dance.

In Matthew 22, Jesus shows us this choreography to recalibrate us back to God's intended dance: "'Love the Lord your God with all your heart and with all your soul and with all your mind.' This is the first and greatest commandment. And the second is like it: 'Love your neighbor as yourself.' All the Law and the Prophets hang on these two commandments."

What is this choreography? What are the steps? They are very simple. Step 1, love God; Step 2, love others; Step 3, love yourself. We need all three steps to successfully dance his dance.

Loving God involves spiritual affection (Ps 42) and ethical living (Jn 14:21). Spiritual affection is displayed in a genuine desire to develop a deeper relationship with God. This happens through time spent in corporate and personal worship. More specifically, spiritual affection is conveyed and cultivated through disciplines like studying God's Word, prayer, fasting, fellowship with other believers, attending church, and serving the community. Ethical living is expressed through obeying God's commands and conforming our character to Christ: social honesty, economic justice, verbal kindness, relational compassion, sexual purity, political civility, and integrity in every aspect of life.

Loving people entails living a life of humility, where we do not think of ourselves more highly than we ought, but rather with sober judgment (Rom 13:3). It also means to seek other people's benefit in all circumstances and to forgive them when they annoy, offend, or injure us.

Loving ourselves involves accepting ourselves the way God made us: physically, mentally, emotionally, and spiritually. It also requires resistance to comparing ourselves to other human beings. Unfortunately, many people have a poor perception of themselves. They embrace unhealthy self-talk like, "I'm so ugly. I'm so fat. I'm so dumb. I can't stand myself!" But who are we to disdain our human vessels, which God created and deemed "good" and worthy temples to hold his Spirit, his image within? If we can't love ourselves, then how can we even begin to love God, who is above time and space, yet ever present within us and his creation? Listen to the apostle Paul's words in Philippians 2:3–4:

> Be free from pride-filled opinions, for they will only harm your cherished unity. Don't allow self-promotion to hide in your hearts, but in authentic humility put others first and view others as more important than yourselves. Abandon every display of selfishness. Possess a greater concern for what matters to others instead of your own interests.

Paul is elaborating on Jesus's simple command to return to the dance: love God and love others as ourselves.

Conclusion

Like those little, wobbly Nutcracker angels, if we look about and take care of our fellow dancers on this stage called "life," rather than running amok for own enjoyment, we will fit seamlessly into the dance. We will participate in creating a harmonious whole, that blesses everyone involved, as the Choreographer intended all along.

This is the essence of God's dance: As his commissioned lords and ladies, he wants us to dance in fellowship with him and in community with others. He wants us to dance domestically and abroad; God's dance is both a local and global dance.

Has the Choreographer got everyone's attention yet? Are we ready to return to the dance? Are we willing to rejoin our divine dance partner? Will we keep our eyes fixed on the Choreographer and follow his every step for our lives? As we continue through the dance of life, may we never lose sight of the Choreographer.

DISCUSSION QUESTIONS

1. Thinking of God as the Choreographer, do you think he's offended, or upset, or frustrated, or hurt, that we've forgotten his dance?
2. Knowing that we've got some "brushing up" to do in remembering the choreography, do you think we're embarrassing ourselves, or others with our neglect?

3. What kind of danger or harm might we be causing by forgetting God's dance? To those around us? To the world?

Spiritual Exercises

1. We can all think of bodily "poses" relevant to worship (raising of hands, lying prostrate, kneeling with head down, silent contemplation with eyes closed and hands folded, etc.) As you think back on a recent experience, challenging or joyous, create bodily poses and movements would capture a glimpse of that experience. Reflect on God's creation of the mysterious connection between emotion and movement in the human body.

2. Whether alone or in a group, come up with poses for a total of six to eight experiences. Then, work (together) to weave those poses into a choreographed dance of life experiences. Choreograph how you would move from one pose or experience to another. Discuss how this experience affected you. Was it challenging? Did it bring up any emotions? Did you feel a sense of release or anxiety? Was it therapeutic or traumatic?

3. Invite a dancer or dance group to perform a liturgical dance during a worship service at your church. Reflect on the dance and discuss it with a group of church members after the worship service.

RESOURCES FOR FURTHER REFLECTION

1. *My Body is the Temple: Encounters and Revelations of Sacred Dance and Artistry* by Stephanie Butler
2. *Moving through the Scriptures: Of Them That Danced* by Rekesha Pittmam
3. *Sole to Soul: A Sacred Dance Journey* by Katheryn E. Mihelick and Andrea Tecza Shearer
4. *And We Shall Learn through the Dance: Liturgical Dance as Religious Education* by Kathleen S. Turner
5. "Making it Stick: How to Remember Choreography," *Dance Spirit*, https://www.dancespirit.com/making-stick-2326466070.html
6. "Jesus as Lord of the Dance," *Biblical Archeological Society*, https://www.biblicalarchaeology.org/daily/people-cultures-in-the-bible/jesus-historical-jesus/jesus-as-lord-of-the-dance/.

Chapter 7

How Long, O Lord
The Art of Poetry

MANNY DAPHNIS

King David in Prayer (c.1637) by Pieter de Grebber

Pieter de Grebber (c.1600—53) was a Dutch Golden Age painter. He was born in Haarlem, Netherlands to an accomplished artistic family. His father, Frans Pietersz de Grebber, taught Pieter and his two brothers Maria and Albert how to paint. Pieter became a member of the Haarlem Guild of St. Lukein in 1632. Throughout his career, he conflated the influences of Utrecht Caravaggistism, Rubens, and Rembrandt, to create his own style of "Haarlem Classicism," which is characterized by a well-organized clarity and light tints.

De Grebbers's painting *King David in Prayer* depicts the story told in 2 Samuel 24 and 1 Chronicles 21 where Satan tempts David to take a census, which was an act of vanity. In remorse, David prays for God's forgiveness, but he still had to face the consequences of his sin. The angel of the Lord holds the symbols of the plagues: a skull for three days of pestilence, a sword for three months of persecution by David's enemies, and empty ears of corn for three years of famine. David picks pestilence and seventy thousand men died. Next to David are his crown and harp. It was from agonizing life experiences like this that David composed many of his psalms.

CALL TO WORSHIP (PSALM 6)

Leader: O LORD, do not rebuke me in your anger or discipline me in your wrath.

People: Be merciful to me, LORD, for I am faint; O LORD, heal me, for my bones are in agony.

Leader: My soul is in anguish. How long, O LORD, how long?

People: Turn, O LORD, and deliver me; save me because of your unfailing love.

Leader: No one remembers you when he is dead. Who praises you from the grave?

People: I am worn out from groaning; all night long I flood my bed with weeping and drench my couch with tears.

Leader: My eyes grow weak with sorrow; they fail because of all my foes.

People: Away from me, all you who do evil, for the LORD has heard my weeping.

Leader: The LORD has heard my cry for mercy; the LORD accepts my prayer.

People: All my enemies will be ashamed and dismayed; they will turn back in sudden disgrace.

HYMN "HOW LONG WILT THOU CONCEAL THY FACE" BY ISAAC WATTS, *THE PSALMS OF DAVID*, 1719.

How long wilt Thou conceal Thy face?
My God, how long delay?
When shall I feel those heav'nly rays
That chase my fears away?

How long shall my poor laboring soul
Wrestle and toil in vain?
Thy word can all my foes control
And ease my raging pain.

See how the prince of darkness tries
All his malicious arts;
He spreads a mist around my eyes,
And throws his fiery darts.

Be Thou my sun, and Thou my shield,
My soul in safety keep;
Make haste, before mine eyes are sealed
In death's eternal sleep.

How would the tempter boast aloud
If I become his prey!
Behold, the sons of hell grow proud
At Thy so long delay.

But they shall fly at Thy rebuke,
And Satan hide his head;
He knows the terrors of Thy look,
And hears Thy voice with dread.

Thou wilt display Thy sovereign grace,
Where all my hopes have hung,
I shall employ my lips in praise
And victory shall be sung.

SCRIPTURE READING (PSALM 13)

How long, Lord? Will you forget me forever?
    How long will you hide your face from me?
How long must I wrestle with my thoughts
    and day after day have sorrow in my heart?
    How long will my enemy triumph over me?
Look on me and answer, Lord my God.
    Give light to my eyes, or I will sleep in death,
and my enemy will say, "I have overcome him,"
    and my foes will rejoice when I fall.
But I trust in your unfailing love;
    my heart rejoices in your salvation.
I will sing the Lord's praise,
    for he has been good to me.

THEOLOGICAL REFLECTION

"In the beginning God created the heavens and the earth. The earth was without form, and void; and darkness was on the face of the deep. And the Spirit of God was hovering over the face of the waters" (Gen 1:1–2).

What followed these initial verses from the creation account was a series of statements that commenced with the phrase "then God said." Then God said let there be light; then God said let there be a firmament in the midst of the waters; then God said let the waters under the heavens be gathered; then God said.

Almost in poetic, rhythmic form, creation went forth. The majestic Lord of the universe from the jump creates and culminates his creation with the command to man, made in his likeness and image, to go forth and have dominion in the earth. The mandate is simple—rule over what's before you and you do so as you follow the rhythm of the pattern of creation set before you.

While for some, this may seem to be a bit of a stretch, the deeper we look, the more we see that our masterful Creator throughout his sacred word incorporates and infuses rhythm, poetry and song as a creative means to present his truths and no one was more versed in this than King David.

David's Background

Before we delve into Psalm 13, we can't help but pause and think about David's story. The power of his psalms are that they give us a deepened insight into David's heart, and by extension, they encourage and motivate us along our respective faith journeys. David, the man after God's own heart (1 Sam 13:14), was the forgotten shepherd boy of Jesse. I can imagine in our modern-day context, David may very well have been an "oops baby" as there seems to be a gap in age between he and his older brothers and as a result as the Lord sends the prophet Samuel to anoint a king from the sons of Jesse—in 1 Samuel 16, David isn't even remembered by his father. Although David developed some incredible skills as a young shepherd boy, most notably a boldness and courage that stemmed from an unmatched dependency upon God, we also see how this parental neglect produced some problems down the road.

After being anointed as the future king of Israel, David steps onto the scene of history and immediately confronts Goliath, the Philistine champion. We all know the story, David with a sling, a rock, and the Holy Ghost defeats Goliath and leads the Israelite army into the routing of the Philistines, which promptly propels this shepherd boy into military prominence (1 Sam 17–18). Nevertheless, jealousy soon ensues from the hands of King Saul, and David finds himself running for his life for quite some time (many scholars say at least a decade, but no one knows for sure).

By the time we get to 2 Samuel 5 when David's reign begins in earnest, we have a thirty-year-old David that has become a hardened survivor, whose dependence upon the Lord has only deepened as he endured not only the constant threats to his life but also senseless betrayal, derision, and even abandonment by those who he sacrificed to help. David had been through the ringer, and it only got worse as he moved into his royal power.

By this point, David was accustomed to suffering, but what soon followed, one wouldn't wish upon even the starkest of enemies. In life, at times, sorrow abounds, and if the weight of our sorrows were not interspersed with temporary moments of rest, we would not survive. As David enters family life, 2 Samuel tells the sordid ordeal of a damaged David who's not only an adulterer, but he also neglects his parental responsibility in dealing with his son Amnon who rapes his half-sister Tamar, the full sister of Absalom. Two years pass and David's neglectful silence leads to Absalom's vengeful murder of Amnon.

The disparaging story continues with Absalom eventually overthrowing his father as king, dying in battle against David's men, and a broken David crying in deep anguish over the loss of his son (2 Sam 13–18). It is not a stretch to connect David's passivity as a father to the fact that he was neglected as a son. Nevertheless, David's profound sorrow left him drowning in a flood of tears: "Then the king was deeply moved, and went up to the chamber over the gate, and wept. And as he went, he said thus: 'O my son Absalom—my son, my son Absalom—if only I had died in your place! O Absalom my son, my son!'" (2 Sam 18:33).

How Long, O Lord?

This backdrop helps us understand Psalm 13, the "*How Long Psalm.*" While the fifth century church father Theodoret claimed that this psalm was written as a response to the Absolom saga, there is no historical evidence linking the two texts. Rather this psalm should be taken for what it is—a lament of utter exasperation. The Psalms (or sacred songs) come in different styles and types but can generally be categorized as lament, praise, or prayer. Comprising the largest book within the designation of poetic books in the canon of scripture, the Psalms are an invaluable resource to the believer.

However, this Psalm, in particular, gives us an unadulterated look at a broken and despondent David. The Psalm begins as follows: "How long, O LORD? Will You forget me forever? How long will You hide Your face from me? How long shall I take counsel in my soul, Having sorrow in my heart daily? How long will my enemy be exalted over me?"

As you look at the four "how longs" one cannot help but hear the emotional charge as the cry of David grows in intensity and desperation with each "how long." The use of parallelism by repeating "how long" serves to add adds greater emphasis upon his emotional state and what you see is a David, who feels abandoned with nowhere else to turn but to God.

Have you ever been there, where your circumstances have felt so overwhelming that all you can do is cry out to the Lord, "How long?" How long do I have to deal with brokenness or suffer with sickness or endure the loss of loved ones, etc. "How long O Lord, how long?" is the refrain that David utters in classic lament ,and if you ever find yourself in the same place as David, know that you are not alone. I've been here far too often at different stages of my life and even now, there's a part of me that cries out, "How long, O Lord?"

In my darkest moments and places, pen and pad have served as a God-given outlet. After the murder of Ahmad Arberry, Breonna Taylor, and George Floyd, I found myself in that very familiar place. And what came forth was my poem "*How Long*":

How Long, O Lord

Our country is broken and so is our world.
Hate begets hate; while government fans its flame
Marginalized, ostracized, incarcerated, lynched
All to perpetuate evil; all to push forth Empire's world.
Rage is what I feel as I ask where is Justice?
Fatigue is what I feel when I ask Lord why us?
Being Black in America automatically condemns us
Insane is what I feel thinking change can happen for us
Embedded in the very fabric of our nation is this complex
That the color of my skin and those of my brethren
Stain us as deficient; inadequate; upon us a hex
Consequently, justice favors blue & white; justice has no garden
I'M TIRED y'all of this modern-day Jim Crow condition
How do we effect change? How do we spur earnest contrition?
Will the blood of the martyr George Floyd finally be sufficient?
Will the systems that fuel racism and inequality finally be overridden?
If justice and righteousness are the foundations of Your throne
Then maybe You're no longer in this broken system.
Maybe You too condemn these bigoted acts of cowardice
As You've made plain you draw near to the broken-hearted.
Justice in America means widespread, systemic upheaval
Justice in America must start with addressing slavery and all of its evil
Three fifths of a human and personal property is at the root
Justice screams right the wrong. Justice calls. How long?
Justice has eyes, ears, hands, and feet.
Justice has children. Justice has a heartbeat
Justice can no longer wait. Justice has waited too long
Justice screams right the wrong. Justice calls. How long?

There's something that happens when a writer writes or a singer sings or a musician plays that cannot be replicated or released in any other way than the God given outlet they've been entrusted with and it's as they do so that both the doer as well as the witness are truly blessed. David finds himself in this exact space and as he starts off with his "how longs" that lay his soul bare before the Lord, he's able to transition into a clarity of request. Here is principle: When we can be transparent with the Lord, we can be clear about what we actually need from him.

So, if we were to outline what we see here, our first point would be that transparency (complete emotional honesty) leads to intimacy. But the second point is just as poignant. As David is able to be emotionally authentic with the Lord, what comes forth is a clear request of the Lord. If you've ever been truly broken, the raw weight of the emotional trauma that you bear causes you to be a bit uncertain at best, and at worst, totally unraveled. Yet as he is transparent with the Lord, intimacy comes forth; he gains a clarity that he didn't have before.

David goes from a desperate refrain of "How long" to a "Consider and hear me and enlighten my eyes." While I may not be able to see, God can illumine the way so I can understand why I'm on this path. The Lord meets us at our point of "how long" to show us the depths of our "how long" so that we might ultimately understand his purposes through our "how long."

The biggest shift happens as the psalm culminates. "How long" becomes "but I have trusted in your mercy." How can trust come about when one's physical circumstances have yet to change? You see, in faith, our circumstances do not dictate our reality, rather it is the one who holds the power over our circumstances who dictates our reality. As a result, the Psalmist goes from desperation to salvation and does so without any indication of an actual change in his predicament. Nevertheless, a radical change in his disposition is undeniably apparent. Maybe the Lord desires the exact same thing for you and me today? How does this happen? According to verse 5, the psalmist has resolved to place his hope and trust in the mercy of the Lord. You get the sense that there is some experience here. He's been through some things with the Lord ,and the Lord's mercy has proven to be reliable and certain.

As the passage continues, we see that the very core of the Psalmist will be glad as God's salvation is assured. God will save you out of your situation as that is simply what he does. Sometimes we need to look at our own history with the Lord and see that he has truly been faithful unto us even in our lowest moments. And finally, in verse 6, when we see the goodness and bountiful nature of God at work, worship unto the Lord is the only response due him. How can we not but sing unto the Lord?

The "How Long" Psalm is a remarkable piece of poetic artistry replete with solid theology. A broken and desperate David crafts for us a three-part offering that over the centuries has been looked at through different vantage points. Today I posit, these three as follows:

a. Transparency leads to intimacy (verses 1–2)

b. Transparency leads to clarity (verses 3–4)

c. Transparency leads to revelation (verses 5–6)

In the midst of your "How Long," may you cry out to the Most High God! He knows precisely where you are; and he is faithful! As we cry out to him he illuminates our path, and we are reminded anew of his mercy, salvation, and goodness.

PRAYER

Eternal Lord, God of mercy and love, we thank you for your sacrificial care for us. Our hope is in you alone. As the storms of life batter our sails, may you teach us to be earnest and transparent with you in order to grow a deepening trust in Your bountiful salvation unto us. Amen.

DISCUSSION QUESTIONS

1. Who are some of your favorite poets? What are some of your favorite poems? What do you like about them? How do they make you feel when you read them?
2. Why is poetry the most emotionally evocative form of literary art? How does poetry move your emotions?
3. Like Psalm 13, how does understanding the author's background and historical context help you interpret the lines of the poem?
4. How have the Psalms ministered to your soul in times of difficulty and darkness?
5. Why do you think the Holy Spirit inspired so much poetry in the Bible?

SPIRITUAL EXERCISES

1. Choose a psalm and read it reflectively! Study its historical background, meditate on its emotional tone, and discern its theological truths. Let God speak to your soul through the words of the psalm. Offer a prayer of response.
2. Try to recompose a psalm in poetic form.
3. Read a collection of poems by one of the great spiritual poets like John Donne, George Herbert, T.S. Eliot, or Christina Rossetti. Contemplate the meaning and ponder their poetic forms.
4. Host a "poetry night" for your church community. Ask people to read and discuss some of their favorite poems.
5. Incorporate poetry into your church's liturgy. Consider adding a "poetry reading" somewhere in worship service, to either prepare for or reflect on the sermon or Eucharist.

RESOURCES FOR FURTHER REFLECTION

1. *A Metrical Psalter: The Book of Psalms Set to Meter for Singing* by Julie and Timothy Tennant
2. *The Psalter as Witness: Theology, Poetry, and Genre* by W. Dennis Tucker Jr. and W. H. Bellinger Jr.
3. *Reflections on the Psalms* by C.S. Lewis
4. *Between Midnight and Dawn: A Literary Guide to Prayer for Lent, Holy Week, and Eastertide* by Sarah Arthur
5. *Praying with John Donne and George Herbert* by Duane Arnold and Richard Harries
6. *Here in Harlem: Poems in Many Voices* by Walter Dean Myers

Chapter 8

The Power of a Song
The Art of Songwriting

TYLER SMITH

King David Playing the Harp (1662) by Peter Paul Rubens and Jan Boekhorst

Flemish artist Peter Paul Rubens (1577–1640) was a prolific and successful master painter, developing his own baroque style that blended renaissance idealism with colorful, dynamic realism. Propelled by a strong Catholic faith and love for classic art, Rubens spent his early career in Italy studying religious paintings of earlier masters while working in the court of an Italian duke. He then settled in his own studio in Antwerp, where he employed several apprentices to keep up with the steady demand for altarpieces, religious paintings, royal portraits, and other commissioned pieces. Late in his career he combined travels for art study with work as a diplomat and spy for the Spanish Hapsburg court.

Jan Boekhorst studied under Rubens at his studio in Antwerp and the two became friends and regular collaborators. Boekhorst developed a baroque style similar to Rubens and finished many of Rubens's paintings after his death.

This painting, titled *King David Playing the Harp*, began under Rubens's brush in 1616, as a study (perhaps for another painting) of an old man's head and shoulders. After Rubens's death in 1640, Boekhorst discovered the panel and was inspired to develop this contemplative figure into a portrait of David, enlarging the piece with two more panels. The finished painting portrays not an idealized and virile subject, as David tended to be represented, but an old man lost in prayerful reflection as he plays his harp. What moves the viewer is not his royal attire, but the marks of age and experience on his face that speak of a life well-lived with God. Though his unkempt hair and beard suggest the slowness of age, David's slender fingers dance across the strings of his instrument. His barely visible eye gazes upward into the distance, drawing our attention, with his, to the One who inspires his song.

CALL TO WORSHIP (PSALM 33:1–5)

Leader: Sing joyfully to the Lord, you righteous; it is fitting for the upright to praise him.

People: Praise the Lord with the harp; make music to him on the ten-stringed lyre.

Leader: Sing to him a new song; play skillfully, and shout for joy.

People: For the word of the Lord is right and true; he is faithful in all he does.

All: The Lord loves righteousness and justice; the earth is full of his unfailing love.

HYMN "THE GOD OF LOVE MY SHEPHERD IS" BY GEORGE HERBERT (1633)

The God of love my shepherd is,
And He that doth me feed;
While He is mine and I am His,
What can I want or need?

He leads me to the tender grass,
Where I both feed and rest;
Then to the streams that gently pass:
In both I have the best.

Or if I stray, He doth convert,
And bring my mind in frame,
And all this not for my desert,
But for His holy name.

Yea, in death's shady black abode
Well may I walk, not fear;
For Thou art with me, and Thy rod
To guard, Thy staff to bear.

Surely Thy sweet and wondrous love
Shall measure all my days;
And as it never shall remove
So neither shall my praise.

SCRIPTURE READING (PSALM 23)

The Lord is my shepherd, I lack nothing.
    He makes me lie down in green pastures,
he leads me beside quiet waters,
    he refreshes my soul.
He guides me along the right paths
    for his name's sake.
Even though I walk
    through the darkest valley,

I will fear no evil,
> for you are with me;
your rod and your staff,
> they comfort me.
You prepare a table before me
> in the presence of my enemies.
You anoint my head with oil;
> my cup overflows.
Surely your goodness and love will follow me
> all the days of my life,
and I will dwell in the house of the Lord
> forever.

THEOLOGICAL REFLECTION

I remember standing next to my mom in church as a boy, gripping the wooden pew in front of me as I belted out songs like "Amazing Grace" and "Shine, Jesus Shine." Through these songs, truths I did not yet understand were planted in my heart. I remember being an angsty teen, sitting with my headphones on, sensing music touch upon unspoken longings for truth, beauty, and love. I remember the songs that my wife and I shared as we fell in love—songs by Paul Simon, Nickel Creek, and Alison Krauss.

Many songs have accompanied me through life. Some songs have even changed my life. And I'm sure the same is true for you. A song can be a flame that melts your heart to repentance and faith. A song can be a ray of light in a dark season. A song can be the valve that releases pent-up tears. With the aid of songs we learn, remember, lament, repent, worship, pray, and vow. God, our artistic Creator, has hard-wired us for songs.

Songwriting is artistic alchemy. Poetry or music alone can move us deeply. But when put together, the resulting beauty is pure gold. A good song resonates with you. It can move you to tears, stop you in your tracks, or pull you up out of your seat in praise. When this happens, you are encountering beauty.

To try to understand the reasons for this, we will consider a song that has resonated with millions through the generations. It is the best-known song written by the best-known songwriter of all time. It has sold billions of copies and been translated into over seven hundred languages. It has been recited by schoolchildren and prayed at the bedsides of the dying. It has been read, sung, studied, memorized, and preached countless times.

This song is Psalm 23, written by king David. I want to look at three things that make this song resonate with us: the beauty of words, the beauty of music, and the beauty of truth. As we look at Psalm 23 on these three levels, I hope we might behold the God-given art of songwriting and glimpse its special power.

The Beauty of Words

If Psalm 23 were a song on the radio today, the lyric would stand alone as a piece of poetry. That has to do not just with the "message" of Psalm 23, but the particular words David used to craft it.

When David wanted to express the peace and security that he felt from being under the Lord's care, he could have simply written it in propositional form, like this: "I can trust God because he always takes care of me and gives me everything I need. He is the one who gives me inner strength when I feel depleted." That would have been perfectly true—and completely forgettable. Instead, David put this truth in beautiful language, like this:

> The Lord is my shepherd, I lack nothing.
> He makes me lie down in green pastures,
> he leads me beside quiet waters,
> he refreshes my soul. (Psalm 23:1–3a)

These words activate the imagination and move the emotions. It's no wonder millions of people around the world can say these verses by heart.

Sometimes we think poetic language should be flowery or embellished. This is not so. The power of poetic language is found in simplicity and specificity. David the songwriter models this expertly in Psalm 23. In Hebrew, the song is only fifty-seven words long. No words are wasted; every word packs a punch. The words are rich with imagery—that is, words that light up our mind's eye with things to see: green grass, glimmering pools of water, dark valleys, the rod and staff, a table, oil.

These images gain even more power through the magic of metaphor. Metaphor takes one thing and equates it with something else: *The Lord is my shepherd*. This metaphor is a verbal picture worth a thousand words. God is the shepherd; we are the sheep. He is responsible for us. We depend on his watchful care and protection. The controlling metaphor of the Lord as a shepherd continues through verse 4. In verse 5, the metaphorical language shifts to that of the Lord as a host, laying a table for us even while enemies surround us, welcoming us into his home. For songwriters such as David, the only way to express such beautiful truths is to use beautiful language. This is, in part, what gives songs their power to move us.

Another songwriter who understood this was Isaac Watts, called "the Godfather of English hymnody," born in 1674. From a young age Watts showed a knack for writing poetry. Once, little Isaac got in trouble for speaking to his father in rhymes. While being disciplined, he cried, "O father, father, pity take / and I will no more verses make!" During this time in England, it was common practice for churches to chant Psalms. Unfortunately, they used archaic, wooden translations, and the tunes were solemn and dreary. As a teenager young Isaac complained to his father that parishioners were sleepy and disengaged with the singing. One day, sick of hearing his son's complaints, Isaac's father challenged him to come up with something better. Isaac took up the challenge, and the following week he presented his first hymn, called "Behold the Glories of the Lamb," a song based on Revelation 5. It was sung in church that Sunday with enthusiastic response.

Isaac Watts went on to compose some 750 hymns, many of which we still sing today, like "Joy to the World" and "When I Survey the Wondrous Cross." Watts was a gifted poet who crafted hymns with rich, resonant language that moved people's hearts, and that could be set to familiar, singable tunes. He harnessed the power of words to restore lyrical beauty to the church's songs.

Think back to the songs that have most changed you. Why do the words move you? How has the songwriter crafted language to tell a story or paint a picture? The next time you listen to music, make it a point to pay attention to the words you are listening to.

The same goes for the songs you sing in worship. Pay attention not only to *what* they say about God but *how* they say it. Thank God for the songwriter who labored to express this truth beautifully. Good songs use the power of words to move us. But words alone are only part of the story. Songs, of course, need music.

The Beauty of Music

The German Reformer Martin Luther wrote about, "...the great and perfect wisdom of God in music, which is, after all, His product and His gift." Luther goes on in his abrasive style, "A person who...does not regard music as a marvelous creation of God must be a clodhopper indeed and does not deserve to be called a human being; he should be permitted to hear nothing but the braying of asses and the grunting of hogs." To put it more mildly: who doesn't love music?

Music is inherently beautiful. It quite literally *moves* us, vibrating our eardrums that turn sound waves into pitch. Music even resonates in our bones. Music is a form of beauty that touches us in a place deeper, or higher, than words alone can reach. Beethoven is said to have called music "the language of God."

We don't know what the music sounded like that accompanied David's song of the divine shepherd in Psalm 23. Was it sung with a lone voice accompanied by harp? Was it sung with choirs? Did it start softly, then build to a crescendo? Musicians through the centuries have interpreted Psalm 23 in their own style and culture, from Gregorian chant to gospel choirs to modern rock. All of these musical forms are beautiful in their own ways.

Brain science sheds light on the reasons that music moves us so deeply and powerfully. Making music, and to a lesser extend listening to music, is a full-brain experience that integrates many of our brain's processes. A part of our brain called the amygdala, known as "emotional memory center," is of particular interest. The amygdala stores pre-verbal and emotional memories, and since music is so intertwined with emotion, we remember songs even when other memories fade. This is why you can still remember a song you learned when you were three years old even though you can't remember where you put your keys five minutes ago.

I once worked at an adult daycare center where many of the elderly participants suffered from Alzheimer's disease or other forms of dementia. Some of these dear men and women could no longer tell you their own name, but when someone struck up "Amazing Grace" on the piano, their eyes lit up and they would start to sing along.

Music is indeed "[God's] product and his gift." But like all of God's gifts, music is easily taken for granted. We often have "background music." How often do we have foreground music? Good music deserves careful listening. Listen to a variety of genres of music—classical, jazz, blues, folk, rock, hip-hop—so that your musical palette expands.

In the evangelical church, which has long elevated pragmatism over beauty, we need to reclaim the gift of music. We can do this by supporting musicians and giving them frequent opportunities to bring their art into the church, including instrumental music that can draw us into worship without words. We should recover the practice of full-throated congregational singing wherever it has been replaced by a worship band performing on stage. As pastor Kevin DeYoung has written, the songs we sing in church should be able to be sung around a hospital bed in fifty years. Certainly, many musical versions of Psalm 23 fit this description.

Songwriting harnesses the beauty of words and the beauty of music. But there is a third essential ingredient in a good song: truth.

The Beauty of Truth

According to the wisdom of country music, a good song is "four chords and the truth." We don't know how many chords David plucked on his harp, but Psalm 23 certainly has the truth. This truth comes from the Holy Spirit's inspiration through David's lived experience.

Picture King David as the old man in Rubens's painting. One day as he gazes out at the hills around Jerusalem, he begins daydreaming. He is back on a scrub-brush dotted hillside as a fourteen-year-old watching his father's flocks. He remembers how much that flock needed his care. How helpless and lost they were without him! How prone they were to wander from safety! How he defended them from predators! With a flash of insight from the Spirit, David sees that *he* is the sheep, and God is his true shepherd. *The Lord is my shepherd.* This deserves a song. David calls for his harp and tunes it up. The wheels are turning, and the thoughts are clicking into place. *Your rod and your staff, they comfort me.* He starts strumming and singing while the royal scribe takes notes. When he is finished, he asks for the tablet, scratches out a line here, adds a line there, finishes a verse there, until at last he sings it through in its full form. He lets out a contented sigh, as if to say, Amen.

There is a saying that "what is most personal is also most universal." This was a deeply personal song for David. It's no surprise that these divinely inspired words about David's relationship with God have continued to resonate with millions. How often have we imagined the Lord as our shepherd, leading us to needed rest or guiding us to safety? How often have we felt the darkest valleys of life closing in around us and felt the rejoinder, *I will not fear, for you are with me*?

We have all had the experience of being deeply moved by a song, even to the point of tears. We've all had the experience of finding a song that gave words to a part of our life that we had yet to name. Maybe it was a hymn or worship song in church. Maybe it was just a song on the radio that reminded you of a special person. When this happens, the truth of the song resonates with the truth of your experience. As songwriters Andrew Peterson and Pierce Pettis sing, "A thing resounds when it rings true / ringing all the bells inside of you." That's the power of a song.

Truth can come in many forms. Just as a painter, sculptor, or poet does not need to be a follower of Jesus in order to create beautiful art, many beautiful, true songs are written by people who are not Christians. There are songs that tell the truth of the human condition: the experiences of falling in love, losing love, longing for home, losing innocence, finding forgiveness, and more. The truth in these songs resonate deeply with us.

The best songs don't merely tell the truth; they *surprise* us with truth. This is what happens in the last few words of Psalm 23. A literal translation of verse 6 would read, "surely goodness and mercy will *chase* me all the days of my life." This is the same word that David has used in other Psalms to describe his enemies pursuing him! David is comforting himself with the fact that God's love will come after him doggedly and relentlessly. David is confessing to God, "I can't outrun your love."

There is no truth more beautiful than this. Psalm 23 reveals the kind of love that will melt a heart of stone, the kind of love that seeks and saves the lost, the kind of love that makes the shepherd leave the ninety-nine to find the stray. This love is found in Jesus Christ, who said, "I am the good shepherd" (John 10).

When a song's truth is rooted in Jesus, the source of all truth and beauty, it will resonate for eternity. After all, it is he who inspired David to write. It is he who spoke this world into being by his powerful word "while the morning stars sang together" (Job 38:7). It is he who determined that music should be one of the first sounds we hear and one of the last memories to fade. Indeed, we sing only because it is the Lord who sings over us with his love (Zeph 3:17). The Lord himself is the power of the song. And someday as we stand before him, the Lamb who was slain for us, the good shepherd who laid his life down for his sheep, all our songs will find their true meaning.

Conclusion

Until then, how are you beholding beauty through songs? Here are some suggestions: immerse yourself in the Psalms, the songbook of the Bible. Make a list of the songs that have been instrumental in your Christian journey and reflect on why and how they have shaped you. Try your hand at writing a song from your own experience. If you aren't musical, find someone who can help you set your song to music.

As someone once said, "writing about music is like dancing about architecture." So here is my attempt to write a song that captures the heart of this message:

"The Power of a Song"
©Tyler Smith, 2020

In churches and at baseball games
In waiting rooms and at cafes
Or when the band gets up to play

You will hear a song
On cassette tapes and 33s
On FM waves and CDs
Though it is bound by none of these
It just lives on and on
Oh, that's the power of a song

It's how I learned my ABCs
How to count by twos and threes
And to say the things I could not speak
When love was young and strong
I've seen people old and gray
Who can't remember their own names
But when that old piano plays
They start singing right along
Oh, that's the power of a song
That's the power of a song

A song can make you laugh or weep
Can pull you up out of your seat
Or lull a baby off to sleep
And make grown-up worries gone
It can tell a story, sing God's praise
Bring home to pilgrims far away
Or meet you in your darkest place
With hope to carry on
Oh, that's the power of a song
That's the power of a song

A song has driven empires to their knees
Delivered hope to captives
And made cynic hearts believe
It even helped to save a wretch like me

So if you've got a song to sing
Then get it out, let it ring
'Cause someone out there's listening
But even if they're not
There's one who all the songs come from
And if you listen close enough
You can hear him singing over us
Like the breaking of the dawn
And he's the power of the song
He's the power of the song
He's the power of the song

PRAYER

Lord, thank you for the incredible gift of songs. Thank you for making us creatures who can behold beauty through music. Thank you for the many songwriters you have inspired to compose songs that have changed us, taught us, encouraged us, and caused us to long for you. Guide us to the songs that are most true and beautiful. We ask this in the name of Jesus, the source of all truth and beauty. Amen.

DISCUSSION QUESTIONS

1. What songs have been instrumental in your Christian journey? Why?
2. Make a list of the songs that have changed your life the most. Why and how did they affect you? Listen to them again.
3. Based on the criteria of truth and beauty, what separates a bad song from a good song? Give an example of a song that affected you negatively.
4. If you were to write a song, what would it be about?

SPIRITUAL EXERCISES

1. Writing about music feels a little like dancing about food; you can only say so much about songs before you have to let songs speak for themselves. Listen to some exceptional songwriters like Rodgers and Hammerstein, Bob Dylan, James Taylor, Paul Simon, Emmylou Harris, Lin-Manuel Miranda, John Prine, Andrew Peterson, Pierce Pettis, or Andy Gullahorn. Think about how the truths in the songs confirm and contradict biblical truth.
2. Host a "listening party" with friends or family. Sit together and listen carefully to a whole album. Discuss which songs move you and why.
3. Attend a concert by a singer-songwriter. Reflect on the differences between a live concert and listening to an album on a device.
4. Find a forgotten hymn and set it to new music. Isaac Watts, Anne Steele, or William Cooper are good places to start. So many of these old hymns are no longer sung in churches, even though they have such well-crafted language and deep theology.

RESOURCES FOR FURTHER REFLECTION

1. *Adorning the Dark* by Andrew Peterson
2. *Resonate: Enjoying God's Gift of Music* by Mark Beuving
3. *Songwriting Without Boundaries: Lyric Writing Exercises for Finding Your Voice* by Pat Pattison
4. *The Second Muse.* This podcast looks at "how songs become songs" featuring interviews with songwriters about their creative process.
5. *Bono and Eugene Peterson Discuss the Psalms.* This twenty-minute video by Fuller Studio films a conversation between Bono, lead singer of U2, and Pastor/Writer/Bible scholar Eugene Peterson. https://www.youtube.com/watch?v=-l4oS5e9oKY.
6. *Country Music* by Ken Burns. This eight-part documentary is an excellent survey of the history of a great American form of songwriting.

Chapter 9

To See What You See
The Art of Popular Music

TIMOTHY BOGERTMAN

Concert at the Gorge by Bill Higginson and Olga Rybalko

The husband-and-wife duo, Bill Higginson and Olga Rybalko, are collaborative artists who currently reside in British Columbia. Their live event paintings bring people together to celebrate the visual arts. The animated artists entertain crowds with their shared vision and synergistic brushwork at concerts, weddings, private parties, and business functions. During events, they try to capture the emotion and meaning of the moment and communicate it to the audience in visual form. They have won first place awards at prestigious art competitions like the Golden Brush and continue to collaborate on a variety of art projects.

In their painting *Concert in the Gorge*, the breathtaking backdrop that surrounds the stage draws viewers into the scene. Each face is turned toward the stage, experiencing the dazzling sights and sounds of the concert that brought the capacity crowd together. Notice how the light washes over the audience, creating a sense that something else is at work in the concert—something transcendent—something sublime and supernatural, which can't be fully explained. There is also a light that emanates from the crowd back to the stage, reminding us of the incarnational encounter between the band and the live audience.

CALL TO WORSHIP (PSALM 40:1–5)

Leader: I waited patiently for the Lord; he turned to me and heard my cry.

People: He lifted me out of the slimy pit, out of the mud and mire; he set my feet on a rock and gave me a firm place to stand.

Leader: He put a new song in my mouth, a hymn of praise to our God.
People: Many will see and fear the Lord and put their trust in him.

Leader: Blessed is the man who makes the LORD his trust, who does not look to the proud, to those who turn aside to false gods.

People: Many, O LORD my God, are the wonders you have done. The things you planned for us no one can recount to you; were I to speak and tell of them, they would be too many to declare.

HYMN "THIS IS MY FATHERS WORLD" BY MALTBIE BABCOCK (1901)

This is my Father's world,
And to my listening ears
All nature sings, and round me rings
The music of the spheres.

This is my Father's world:
I rest me in the thought
Of rocks and trees, of skies and seas—
His hand the wonders wrought.

This is my Father's world:
The birds their carols raise,
The morning light, the lily white,
Declare their Maker's praise.

This is my Father's world:
He shines in all that's fair;
In the rustling grass, I hear Him pass,
He speaks to me everywhere.

This is my Father's world.
O let me ne'er forget
That though the wrong
Seems oft so strong,
God is the ruler yet.

This is my Father's world:
The battle is not done:
Jesus who died shall be satisfied,
And earth and Heav'n be one.

SCRIPTURE READING (ACTS 17:16–23)

While Paul was waiting for them in Athens, he was greatly distressed to see that the city was full of idols. So he reasoned in the synagogue with both Jews and God-fearing Greeks, as well as in the marketplace day by day with those who happened to be there. A group of Epicurean and Stoic philosophers began to debate with him. Some of them asked, "What is this babbler trying to say?" Others remarked, "He seems to be advocating foreign gods." They said this because Paul was preaching the good news about Jesus and the resurrection. Then they took him and brought him to a meeting of the Areopagus, where they said to him, "May we know what this new teaching is that you are presenting? You are bringing some strange ideas to our ears, and we would like to know what they mean." (All the Athenians and the foreigners who lived there spent their time doing nothing but talking about and listening to the latest ideas.)

Paul then stood up in the meeting of the Areopagus and said: "People of Athens! I see that in every way you are very religious. For as I walked around and looked carefully at your objects of worship, I even found an altar with this inscription: to an unknown god. So you are ignorant of the very thing you worship—and this is what I am going to proclaim to you."

THEOLOGICAL REFLECTION

"That was, by far, the best concert I ever attended. Absolutely amazing!" My friend John uttered these words at the conclusion of the U2 concert in New York City in the autumn of 2001, when our nation was reeling from the immanent September 11th terrorist attacks. The impact was especially palpable in New York, the ground zero of the attacks.

As longtime U2 fans, we knew that Bono (the lead singer) would offer words of hope for our hurting hearts. And sure enough, the music was soulful, the lights and colors were spectacular, and every song in the set was chosen with poignant purpose. The band members were like priests enacting liturgies of lament and consolation to thousands of bewildered and grief-stricken fans that night, singing songs that reflected universal truth and beauty and resonated with every soul in the audience. As theologian Steve Garber commented about attending a U2 concert during his 2012 commencement address at Geneva College, "Listening to him [Bono] that night I was once again reminded of the unusual gift that is his, viz. he sings songs that are shaped by the truest truths of the universe, in a language the whole world can understand."[1]

As Christians, John and I sensed the Holy Spirit moving through the seats at Madison Square Garden that night. Although most of the fans were oblivious to the existence of the Holy Spirit, they recognized that they were in the presence of something transcendent—something bigger and beyond themselves—something beautiful beyond description. Bono understood it! He even said, "The Spirit's in the house!"

Some Christians may consider this statement blasphemous. How can the Spirit of God move through a rock concert? They've been taught that God doesn't like rock music, or for that matter, any "secular" music. They have adopted the belief that God can only be present when the artist is a Christian and sings Christian songs.

Consequently, these Christians caution their fellow believers from listening to any music that doesn't convey an explicitly Christian worldview. They draw sharp lines between the sacred and the secular, arguing that "non-Christian" music is a bad spiritual influence and harmful to the soul. They believe that God can only be honored and worshipped through

---

1. Garber, "Singing Songs that the Whole World Can Hear."

material and music with a Christian message. Thus, they conclude that since "secular" music does not glorify God, Christians should avoid it altogether.

But is it possible for Christians (and everyone) to encounter truth in songs by popular musicians like Elvis Presley, the Beetles, Led Zeppelin, Marvin Gaye, and Aretha Franklin? Can we behold true beauty when listening to songs by Michael Jackson, Madonna, Garth Brooks, and Eminem? How about more modern musical artists like The Black Keys, Arcade Fire, Kendrick Lamar, and Lady Gaga? How can anyone hear God's voice while Miley Cyrus is twerking on stage? But lest we forget, God has already established the improbable precedent of speaking through an ass (Num 22)! Perhaps this is a case where the old proverb is apropos: "Don't throw the baby out with the bathwater!"

On the other hand, we should be honest about the fact that most pop music is engaged haphazardly. As we seek to be entertained, we can uncritically consume the values and philosophies the musician is expressing, many of which are profane or sacrilegious to Christian sensibilities. Most of us have our favorite music that we listen to while riding in the car, working out in the gym, or relaxing with friends—we listen to more popular music than we realize. But do we ever pause to consider how these messages may be shaping our hearts, minds, and souls?

Therefore, it is prudent to ask: Can pop music make meaningful contributions to our lives, or is it just mindless entertainment that leads our souls down a dark and dangerous path? Is the potential reward of discovering unexpected truth and beauty worth the risk of exposing ourselves to that which is unholy? In Acts 17:16-23, the apostle Paul shows us how we can engage culture and encounter truth and beauty even in a city full of idols.

Shock and Awe—Idols everywhere!

In Acts 17:16, the apostle Paul's missionary journey brought him to Athens. While he was waiting for Silas and Timothy to join him there, he began wandering through the city streets. After all, Athens was a tourist attraction for people throughout the Roman Empire. Pilgrims traveled far and wide to see the wonders of the ancient world—the Acropolis, the Parthenon, and a host of other Hellenistic sites.

As Paul passed through the pantheistic temples, he was frozen in a state of shock and awe. His heart was appalled and even provoked to the point of anger as he gazed upon the idols of antiquity. As a former Pharisee and current follower of Jesus Christ, he was a committed monotheist, and he was well aware of the Old Testament teachings about the dangers of idolatry.

Paul's reaction to the idols of Athens is similar to the way some modern Christians respond to modern pop music. When we hear music or see videos that celebrate the idols of lust, greed, and vanity (to name a few), and we immediately reject what we hear. Sometimes, this is the right reaction. As followers of Jesus, we must learn to love the things of God, and to hate what God hates. Noticing and naming idols is an important exercise in spiritual discretion. It helps us understand the ungodly lies that have influenced the way we live.

But what if Paul just stopped here and returned to his ship? With so many idols lining the streets, it would have been easy for him to shake the pagan dust off his sandals and move on to a city that shared his own beliefs and values. But Paul did not retreat or run away! He continued to engage the Athenians, seeking to understand the culture of the place God called him and looking for opportunities to preach the good news about Jesus and his resurrection.

Seeking to Understand

After Paul reasoned with Jews and God-fearing Greeks at the synagogue, he wound up debating with some philosophers in the marketplace. Athens was a known educational center, renowned for its deep roots in the subjects of politics, philosophy, and rhetoric. Famous philosophers like Socrates, Plato, and Aristotle had risen to prominence in this city. Athenians loved to hear and discuss new ideas.

As Paul shared the gospel, a group of Epicurean and Stoic philosophers began to dispute with him. Epicureanism was a form of hedonism, the belief that emphasized the pursuit of pleasure and the avoidance of pain as the ultimate good. Ironically, this ancient philosophy is still alive and well today; and it's a common theme in modern pop music. For instance, consider the opening line of the 1977 song "Sex, Drugs, and Rock 'n' Roll" by the English band Ian Dury and the Blockheads: "Sex and drugs and rock and roll is all my brain and body need. . ." Twenty years later, pop/rock musician Sheryl Crow epitomized Epicurean philosophy in the catchy chorus: "If it makes you happy, it can't be that bad."

Stoicism, on the other hand, taught that true meaning and happiness could only be achieved by accepting the moment as it presents itself, by not allowing oneself to be controlled by the desire for pleasure or fear of pain, and by working together and treating others fairly and justly. People cannot control what happens to them; they can only control how they respond to what happens. This philosophy is reflected in Bruce Hornsby's 1986 song

"That's Just the Way It Is." The sarcastic refrain "That's just the way it is, some things will never change" is repeated throughout the song to reflect the stoic philosophy that so many modern people have embraced about politics and racial and economic justice (it is rather ironic that we are still dealing with the same societal problems thirty-five years after this song hit the airways.) But instead of running away from the popular philosophies of his day, Paul actively engaged them with the gospel. He was willing to seek and celebrate common ground, but when it was necessary, he was courageous to confront them with the truth of Jesus Christ.

When we listen to popular music, we enter one of the philosophical arenas of our age. Sometimes, the philosophies are congruent with our Christian values, and other times, they conflict with them, but there is always something to learn. Like other artforms, every piece of pop music communicates something about truth and beauty. If we listen with discerning hearts and minds, we may discover truth and beauty in unlikely places. But how should we do this?

We begin by asking how the music makes us feel. Lyrics are important, but this is not the best starting place. As James K.A. Smith says in his book *You Are What You Love*, "What if, instead of starting from the assumption that human beings are thinking things, we started from the conviction that human beings are first and foremost lovers?"[2] What sort of emotion does this music make me feel—love, anger, sadness, fear, or joy? Often the songs that resonate with our souls have a melodic sound or instrumental quality and that affects us on a heart level. When the song comes on, our toes start tapping, maybe we air-drum on the steering wheel, and we find ourselves humming or singing along with the sound.

Once we've reflected on how the song makes us feel, then we can begin to examine how the lyrics shape our thinking. Just as Paul engaged the philosophies of his time, so we can engage our culture's most current ideas by listening to pop music. Few art forms can capture the philosophies of the day as quickly or crafty. When Lady Gaga sings "I'm on the right track baby, I was born this way," she distills one of the prevailing philosophies of our age into a few clever lines. Her song asserts that there is nothing wrong with the way a person feels or thinks about their life or sexuality. I was born to love and live a certain way, and there is nothing wrong with that. But Christians know that, even though all humans are made in the image of God, sin has distorted our thoughts and desires.

While we can agree with Lady Gaga that we bear the image of our Creator we must recognize that sin has tainted who we love and how we live.

---

2. Smith, *You Are What You Love*, 7.

Our sinful hearts are deceitful and often lead us astray (Jer 17:9), derailing us from following the path of God's will. But if we thoughtfully engage the theology in the pop song, we will eventually see how it shapes our thinking. What is this music saying about me? How is it moving toward or away from God? How does it speak to the spirit and age in which we live? As we answer these questions, we may see truth and beauty from a new perspective, or we might find the same old idolatry that has been peddled throughout the generations.

After we have considered how the music makes us feel and how it shapes our thinking, we can listen and share with others in community. Just as Paul had direct dialogue with the philosophers of his day, we can have discussions with the artists of our day. Likewise, as Paul had constant conversation with his ministry colleagues, we can have conversations with confidants in our own lives. When we play a song or attend a concert, we don't have to do it alone—we can listen or go with a friend. We can listen to a pop song and then take time to discuss it with someone. I have often missed the point or misinterpreted the message of a song, but afterward, a friend opened my eyes to the depth and beauty of it. Having a conversation after a performance creates an opportunity to reflect on the significance of what we have seen and heard. It allows us to sift through the sand and find the hidden gems of beauty.

Finding Common Ground: Truth and Beauty in a Pluralized World

While the Epicurean and Stoic philosophers struggled to make sense of Paul's preaching, they invited him to the Areopagus ("high city") to explain these new and strange ideas. They wanted to hear more and engage in deeper dialogue.

There, Paul stood up and addressed a large crowd. Knowing how disturbed Paul was earlier, we might expect him to stand up and shout, "You are all idolaters, and your judgment is close at hand unless you repent!" But Paul started with a wiser approach. He began by finding common ground and searching for places where truth can be found in their life. He affirmed their religious devotion and pointed out the fact that he found their alter with the inscription to an unknown God. Later in his speech (in verse 28), he quoted two Greek poets and connected their message with the hope of the gospel.

Paul listened carefully and paid attention to the art and philosophy of the Greeks. As he viewed their art and studied their philosophy, he found much of it offensive and profane. Yet he kept searching for aspects of truth and beauty that he could affirm, and he kept looking for contact points that could become bridges to the gospel. Like twentieth century theologian Karl Barth purportedly said, "with the Bible in one hand, and the newspaper in the other."[3] But in Paul's case, it was with the Bible in one hand, and the art and poetry of Athens in the other. His willingness to engage in open and honest dialogue earned him the credibility to preach about the death and resurrection of Jesus Christ. When the crowd heard the scandalous word "resurrection," some of them sneered, but others wanted to hear more on the subject. A few people, among them a man named Dionysius and a woman named Damaris, became believers.

Can the same be said of us as we listen to popular art? Is the pop music of our time just an empty shell of mind-numbing entertainment, or is it a hidden treasure chest of truth and beauty? We must concede that popular music sometimes has a syrupy sweetness to it; it tastes good going down but leaves little substance. But if we keep searching for God's truth, even in places far from him, we just might find it.

John Calvin once wrote "As truth is most precious, so all men confess it to be so. And yet, since God alone is the source of all good, you must not doubt, that whatever truth you anywhere meet with, proceeds from Him, unless you would be doubly ungrateful to Him."[4] If this is true, when we hear pop songs (whether it be Rock, Rap, Metal, Country, R&B, Bluegrass, Hip Hop or Jazz) we can look for the ways the artist points to something that is true and good even if they don't fully understand it themselves. Like Paul, we should grieve over the rampant idolatry in our world, but we might also see how a pop song points to a universal truth that draws someone closer to Christ's kingdom.

But can the same be said for beauty? When we hear a song that stirs our hearts and draws us closer to God, can we see that this beauty belongs to God? Isn't this why we want to share some of our favorite songs with others? We want others to behold the same beauty that we see in the song.

Bruce Springsteen is one of my favorite musicians. Why do I find his music so beautiful? It can be hard-driving at times, soft and acoustic at others—he is a talented guitarist, pianist, and harmonica player—but most of all, his songs tell powerful stories that resonate with average blue-collar working-class Americans. His songs are not "Christian" in the narrow sense

---

3 Seat, "Bible and the Newspaper," *Word and Way*, https://wordandway.org/2020/05/05/the-bible-and-the-newspaper/.

4 Calvin, "Letter CCXXXVI," 198–99.

of the term, but they are gospel-centered in the sense that they testify to great truths of human brokenness and the hope of redemption.

When Springsteen sings his evocative song "My Hometown" he not only exposes his own memories of growing up in the small town of Freehold, New Jersey, but he invites his listeners to consider the importance of a theology of place—the mystery and meaning of God placing us in our own hometowns—with all of the nostalgic pain and pleasure, loneliness, and love, and yes, brokenness and beauty. Although the song recounts a specific example of the racial tensions he experienced as a teenager in his hometown, the lyrics capture the universal reality of racism, gun violence, and unemployment that still haunts America's streets over a half century later.

You may love where you grew or where you live now, but you may also feel chained to the inescapable darkness on the edge of town. As my own parents recently moved away from my hometown, I took my son with me to help them pack their belongings. As we pulled away for the last time, I played "My Hometown" on the car stereo. Why did I choose this song for that moment? Because its truth and beauty resonated with my soul in an indescribably spiritual way. Artists like Bruce Springsteen do this for us if we take the time to listen. The best pop songs can usher us into moments like this. They connect our lives to the lives of others. They speak truth and beauty to people from all walks of life. And they have spiritual power beyond their stated purpose—they can help us to see what God sees.

Conclusion

Walker Percy once said, "Bad books always lie. They lie most of all about the human condition."[5] The same can be said for bad pop songs. They lie about who we are as humans. Some popular songs contain appalling lyrics, offensive phrases, and profane images. Like the apostle Paul, we can sometimes be shocked at first glance, but let's keep listening and looking for what God is doing in our midst.

So, whether you attend a concert, turn the dial in your car, or push play on your phone, listen with a mind of discernment and a heart of compassion. And remember that every square inch of this world belongs to God.

> This is my Father's world. O let me ne'er forget.
> That though the wrong seems oft so strong, God is the ruler yet.
> This is my Father's world. The battle is not done.
> Jesus who died shall be satisfied, and earth and Heav'n be one.

---

5 Percy, *Signposts in a Strange Land*, 251.

DISCUSSION QUESTIONS

1. What are some of your favorite popular music songs? Why?
2. Where do you find truth and beauty in these songs?
3. How do you engage with popular music that you find offensive? How should we engage with it? Can there be something redemptive there?
4. With whom could you consume pop music with and have a meaningful conversation about it?
5. Could you ever incorporate pop music into a worship service, sermon, devotional, or Bible study? If so, how would you do it?

SPIRITUAL EXERCISES

1. Make a mix of songs that you think a friend or co-worker might enjoy. Let them know about a few songs that you appreciated on the mix. Ask them if they would make one for you as well. Sharing good music with others can be a way to bless others and to share with them.
2. Attend a concert with someone who might enjoy the same type of music. Go to the concert and engage in the sight, sounds, lyrics, and things that happened there. Afterwards, take some time to discuss what was true, beautiful, or broken about what you just experienced. These conversations afterwards can be very meaningful.
3. Once or twice a week, take some time in the car, at the gym or in the office to listen to pop music that you find engaging and beautiful. These can be moments that bring beauty or joy into the mundane of everyday tasks or activities.

RESOURCES FOR FURTHER REFLECTION

1. *The Day Alternative Music Died* by Adam Caress
2. *The Soul of Hip Hop: Rims, Timbs, and a Cultural Theology* by Daniel White Hodge
3. *Personal Jesus: How Popular Music Shapes Our Souls* by Clive Marsh and Vaughan S. Roberts
4. *Broken Hallelujah: Why Popular Music Matters to Those Seeking God* by Christian Scharen

5. *The Day Metallica Came to Church: Searching for the Everywhere God in Everything* by John Van Sloten

Chapter 10

The Story of God in One Meal

The Art of the Novel

Richard J. Harrington

An illustration to Fyodor Dostoyevsky's *Crime and Punishment* (1880's) by Nikolay Karazin

Nikolay Nikolaevich Karazin (1842–1908) was a Russian military officer, painter, and writer. He graduated from the Moscow cadet school in 1862 and then studied at the Imperial Academy of Arts in Saint Petersburg from 1865–67. After his retirement from a decorated military career, he turned his attention to art. He wrote adventures and ethnographic stories and novels. Later, he became known mostly as a painter and illustrator. He painted many large canvases devoted to battles and especially military actions in Turkestan. He was a prolific book illustrator and a notable author of postcards.

In this graphic illustration, Karazin depicts the dramatic moment in Fyodor Dostoyevsky's novel *Crime and Punishment* when the protagonist, Rodion Raskolnikov kills Alyona Ivanovna, a suspicious old pawnbroker who hoards money and is merciless to her patrons. Lurking behind the door, with the hatchet still in hand, Raskolnikov feels compelled to kill Alyona's innocent and unsuspecting sister, Lizaveta, to protect himself from being identified as the murderer. This indiscriminate act sends his tormented soul on a haunting journey in search of redemption.

CALL TO WORSHIP
(REVELATION 21:1–4; GLORY BE)

Leader: Then I saw a new heaven and a new earth, for the first heaven and the first earth had passed away, and the sea was no more.

People: And I saw the holy city, new Jerusalem, coming down out of heaven from God, prepared as a bride adorned for her husband.

Leader: And I heard a loud voice from the throne saying: Behold, the dwelling place of God is with man. He will dwell with them, and they will be his people, and God himself will be with them as their God.

People: He will wipe away every tear from their eyes, and death shall be no more, neither shall there be mourning, nor crying, nor pain anymore, for the former things have passed away.

All: Glory be to the Father, and to the Son, and to the Holy Ghost, as it was in the beginning, is now, and ever shall be, world without end. Amen. Amen.

HYMN "I LOVE TO TELL THE STORY" BY KATHERINE HANKEY (1866)

I love to tell the story
Of unseen things above
Of Jesus and his glory
Of Jesus and his love

I love to tell the story
Because I know 'tis true
It satisfies my longings
As nothing else can do

I love to tell the story
'Twill be my theme in glory
To tell the old, old story
Of Jesus and his love

I love to tell the story
For those who know it best
Seem hungering and thirsting
To hear it like the rest

And when in scenes of glory
I sing the new, new song
'Twill be the old, old story
That I have loved so long

I love to tell the story
'Twill be my theme in glory
To tell the old, old story
Of Jesus and his love

SCRIPTURE READING (MATHEW 26:26–29)

While they were eating, Jesus took bread, and when he had given thanks, he broke it and gave it to his disciples, saying, "Take and eat; this is my body."

Then he took a cup, and when he had given thanks, he gave it to them, saying, "Drink from it, all of you. This is my blood of the covenant, which is poured out for many for the forgiveness of sins. I tell you, I will not drink from this fruit of the vine from now on until that day when I drink it new with you in my Father's kingdom."

THEOLOGICAL REFLECTION

A novel is a story, usually a long and complex story with many characters, multiple settings, and an overarching meta-narrative that flows through a connected sequence of events. Novels typically follow a narrative arc which begins with introductory background information, then moves to an initial confrontation and rising conflict and then builds to a climax. After the climax, the story shifts to resolution and eventually comes a conclusion. Although fiction, novels deal with real human experience and emotion, and they explore themes that transcend their own internal world.

For example, *Crime and Punishment*, the novel by the Russian author Fyodor Dostoevsky, is the second of Dostoyevsky's novels following his decade-long exile to Russian Siberia and perhaps rivaled in popularity only by his novel, *The Brothers Karamazov*. *Crime and Punishment* was first published in monthly segments in 1866 by the literary journal *The Russian Messenger*. As a single volume, following the—at times—torturous inner struggle of the young Raskolnikov and his horrific crime, many have found timeless themes of God, morality, and redemption within its pages. It has been translated into multiple languages and has become an indisputable classic of prose literature. Numerous students have worked their way through its pages either for an assignment or merely for the pleasure of reading a great story.

Like a novel, the Bible is also a story. It is an overarching meta-narrative of history. Let's look at the parallels. First, it is a book: it has an opening, a middle and an end. With novels in particular this means a beginning, a climax and a conclusion. When we read a novel, what are we looking for? We want to see interesting characters, an exciting adventure, powerful themes and a satisfying conclusion. What do *The Lord of the Rings*, *A Tale of Two Cities* and *Pride and Prejudice* have in common? We might also add, every good John Grisham or Stephen King novel? There is a beginning that introduces us to the characters and presents us with a tension that demands resolution. There is a climax, in which that tension is resolved. In the end, there is a conclusion that brings the story to a satisfying closure. Every story (including every novel) dimly reflects the great story of the Bible, the story of God.

Our Story has a Beginning

Good novels have a good beginning. They get your attention. They start you off on the journey. Dickens begins *A Tale of Two Cities* with perhaps the most identifiable opening line in English literature, "It was the best of times, it was the worst of times."[1] Who would not recognize the start of *The Hobbit*? "In a hole in the ground there lived a hobbit. Not a nasty, dirty, wet hole, filled with the ends of worms and an oozy smell, nor yet a dry, bare, sandy hole with nothing in it to sit down on or to eat: it was a hobbit-hole, and that means comfort."[2] Most will recognize Jane Austen's signature work, *Pride and Prejudice*, by her opening statement: "It is a truth universally acknowledged, that a single man in possession of a good fortune, must be in want of a wife."[3]

The beginning introduces you to the key characters. There is the protagonist. This may be a truly good hero, such as Harry Potter or Frodo Baggins. It might be an anti-hero, such as Dostoyevsky's Raskolnikov. Soon we meet the antagonist: the villain, Dark Lord, or something more nebulous but equally sinister. Tension and conflict arises; it needs resolution. Raskolnikov commits his heinous act murdering the pawnbroker and her sister Lizaveta. His inner guilt of getting away with the crime begins to drive him seemingly insane. The Ring of Power is identified and needs to be taken to the fires of Mount Doom to be unmade. Mitch McDeere joins a law firm that he cannot leave because it is run by the mob! The tension builds until a breaking point: Potter versus Voldemort; Edmond the traitor and the White Witch; Mr. Darcy's pride set against Elizabeth Bennett's prejudice. It is heading towards a climax.

Likewise, when Jesus celebrated communion with his disciples on the night before he was crucified, he didn't create the sacrament from scratch. He brought the ordinance in to the great metanarrative of the Bible. He celebrated Passover, which is found in the Torah, the first five books of the Bible and the account of the theological start of God's people Israel. The Torah sets us off with God as creator, introduces us to the patriarchs, leads to Israel's bondage in Egypt, takes them out through a mighty exodus towards the Promised Land, and ends with The Law given on Sinai that defines the People of God.

---

1 Dickens, *Tale of Two Cities*, 1.
2 Tolkien, *Hobbit*, 1.
3 Austen, *Pride and Prejudice*, 273.

Passover in particular was a defining feast. The bitter herbs brought out the bitterness of slavery, while the unleavened bread symbolized the call to purity. The four cups of wine represented God's special calling upon Israel: "I will bring out," "I will deliver," "I will redeem," and "I will take" (Exod 6:6–7). The head of the household would, in a sense, annually remind the family at this meal, "We are part of this narrative and characters in God's story."

What is the introduction to God's story? It begins with a bang—a really big one! "In the beginning, God" creates all things and brings order out of chaos. He puts humanity, the story's anti-hero, into a garden of beauty. There is only one true protagonist in God's story and that is the Lord himself. It doesn't take long before we meet the story's primary antagonist, slithering through the shrubbery and tempting the young couple to transgress. The judgment of sin is death, set by God from the introduction. Minor characters fill its chapters, but the ongoing battle between God alongside his anti-hero, Man, facing off with Satan and his sinful rebellion can be found on every page.

The tension builds and builds: human beings keep failing, sinning, breaking God's commands and dying. It reaches a breaking point when Jesus Christ comes into the story. The powers of darkness grow fiercer. By the time Jesus celebrates this last supper, Satan and sin are in full force. The Dark Lord has shown himself and the Prince of Peace is ready to defeat him.

As Christians, I am convinced we have the best story of the world to tell. We sometimes call this our worldview. It is a story filled with meaning, purpose, and value. It is a story in which all human beings are made in the image of God. It's a story in which the tension of sin is real, and exists not just "out there," but inside every human heart. Our antagonist is gathering up his dark forces to deceive and destroy. A resolution is needed.

It is not the only story people tell. There is the story that we are no more than the products of chance and time. There is a story of might makes right, of vapid materialism, or of a universe devoid of meaning or purpose. But this story is different. It echoes throughout history about a world that started with a Storyteller seeing all that he has made and declaring, "It is very good," and making sure it ends up that way.

Our Story has a Climax

The climax of a novel is the story's heart. It is "the moment in a novel at which the crisis comes to its point of greatest intensity and is then resolved. It is also the peak of emotional response from a reader, and it usually represents the turning point in the action." In the climax, the story has reached its apex, culmination, summit! This is why we read novels, to experience the thrill of the climax. The Ring of Power is thrown into Mt. Doom. Mr. Darcy proposes to Miss Bennett. Raskolnikov confesses to his crime: "It was I who killed the old pawnbroker woman and her sister Lizaveta with an axe and robbed them."[4]

We love a good fight scene, a war story, a battle of good triumphing over evil. Perhaps the greatest stories involve sacrificial love. Aslan, the Great Lion, dies for the traitor, Edmond. Harry Potter is a horcrux and must be destroyed in order to vanquish Voldemort. Carton goes to the guillotine instead of Darnay. The antagonist thinks he or she won, but no, the sacrifice is what saves!

In *A Tale of Two Cities*, Charles Darnay is the nephew of the wicked Marquis St. Evremonde. It is revealed at one point that the marquis and his brother kill a peasant after violating his sister. Before he dies, the peasant curses the marquis and his descendants with "the mark of the red cross."[5] Even Charles Darnay's mother says of him as a baby, "I have a presentiment that if no other innocent atonement is made for this, it will one day be required of him." On the day it is required, his friend Sydney Carton who possesses the providential coincidence of looking very similar to Darnay, takes his place and his death. It is Darnay's substitutionary atonement.

When Jesus celebrates Passover, he applies it to himself. He tells us to take and eat the bread as his body. This meal is no longer just about an exodus from Egypt out of slavery. The cup is the blood of a new covenant. A new chapter is beginning! This was likely the third cup, the cup of redemption. It is poured out for the forgiveness of sins. The paschal lamb is replaced by a new sacrifice, the Lamb of God. The final plague of the death of the firstborn is fulfilled as it falls on the firstborn Son of God. He is our "innocent atonement" and the one who takes the "red cross" for us. It is as if Jesus is saying, a resolution to the story of God is coming to a head. "Something major is happening, and it is happening now."

The metanarrative of the Bible has a climax. It is the cross of Calvary. In Acts 3:15, Peter preaches, "You killed the Author of life, whom God raised from the dead." It is as if Charles Dickens entered into one of his stories, as if J. R. R. Tolkien found his way into Middle Earth, as if Dostoyevsky became a protagonist in his fictional Russian worlds, and then died to redeem his characters.

Why do Christians obsess about the cross? Because it is the greatest act of love. It is God's redemption. More than that, there is a resurrection

---

4 Dostoyevsky, *Crime and Punishment*, 417.
5 Dickens, *Tale of Two Cities*, 348.

to follow! The empty tomb remains the symbol of triumph, victory, and resolution to our great plight against death. It is not just another chapter of the story; it is our story's climax.

As Christians, we live after the climax of the metanarrative. The Dark Lord is defeated. The protagonist has overcome. As those united to Jesus Christ, we get to enjoy grace. We live in gratitude. The tension is over, the battle is won, the story has culminated. We live in the aftermath. We spend our lives in the spoils of his victory. Enjoy it! Celebrate it! More than that, we get to be emissaries of this good news. Proclaim it! Be bearers of the gospel, for "It is finished!"

Our Story has a Conclusion

After the story's climax, a novel is not done. After Frodo destroys the ring, what happens next? The Peter Jackson movies leave it out, but the hobbits must go back to the Shire and retake it from evil. Mr. Darcy's proposal doesn't end *Pride and Prejudice*. We still enjoy the wedding and a few words about their ongoing love and relationship. The reader needs a moment to celebrate and rejoice, to take it all in. Oftentimes, there is a recognition of character development. Bilbo, Frodo, Edmond, Darcy, Elizabeth, Harry Potter, Mitch, Darnay are no longer the same people. They have changed, for the better. *Crime and Punishment* requires an epilogue in which Raskolnikov goes to Siberia and eventually is redeemed by the persevering and unconditional love of Sonya.

If a writer blows the ending, she may ruin the story. The narrative cannot end too abruptly; it must ease into the final page, the last sentence, the concluding word. The story of God isn't over yet. Obviously, human beings are still around after Jesus's resurrection, and it has been two millennia and ticking. We are somewhere in the book's pages, awaiting the story's conclusion. There is even more character development to come for each of us. The Holy Spirit is doing his work of sanctification, making us like Jesus Christ, as we wait for the last trumpet.

Jesus doesn't end this Passover without a whisper of what is to come. He tells us he won't drink the fruit of the vine again until he drinks it anew with us in his father's kingdom. The day will come when we all will dine together at the Great Wedding Feast of the Lamb. The Father's Kingdom, the rule and reign of God, has been inaugurated in the death and resurrection of Jesus Christ, but will be absolute on his return.

This final cup may refer to the fourth and final cup of wine taken during Passover, the *Hallel* cup or the cup of praise. Could it be that Jesus lifted the fourth cup, spoke of this coming time, then put it back down as he delays the final celebration a while longer? The conclusion will have to wait a few more pages as the story continues.

The conclusion has been long foreshadowed, certainly in the Book of Revelation, but other passages also, such as the Olivet discourse (Matt 24; Mark 13; Luke 21) and the epistles 1 and 2 Thessalonians. Yes, the serpent's head is crushed, but he is still writhing. Sin has been defeated, but it is still in our hearts. We are waiting for a blissful ending.

We know that the story will conclude with a happily ever after. The white rider comes and he will right all wrongs. The groom will be united with his bride forever. Human beings will once again flourish with the guilt and shame of sin forever behind us. The Dark Lord will be banished from paradise without end.

As Christians there is always reason for hope, for we know how the story will end. Hopelessness and despair are part of a different story of the world. Hope is how our story reads. No matter how broken the world may seem, or ugly sin may show itself, the conclusion is coming.

We will experience and enjoy a new heaven and a new earth, free of sin, suffering, Satan and sickness. We will enjoy the New Jerusalem with God as our light. Every tear will be wiped away and the tree of life accessible to all who dwell there.

The gloominess of cultural decay or the ugliness of political partisanship can be draining on our hearts. Interpersonal conflicts, nagging temptations, past sins and failures can be utterly disheartening. Living with our eyes set on our momentary trials leads to despondency. But when we lift our eyes to the great metanarrative of Scripture and the hope of eternal life to come, we are lifted out of our slough of despond and set free from the prison of giant despair to enjoy the upcoming celestial city! Like Christian in *Pilgrim's Progress*, we are on a journey that has a distinct destination and setting our hope firmly there will fill us with anticipation and joy!

Conclusion

Jesus told the Story of God in one meal. He relayed the narrative of our reason for being in one supper. Today we call it Communion, Eucharist, the Last Supper or the Lord's Table. Like every story, God's Story has a beginning, a climax, and a conclusion and we as his people get to play a role.

The final chapter is coming, but what next? Is this the only story we are in? Far from it. As C. S. Lewis said in the final pages of the seventh book of *The Chronicles of Narnia*, "Now at last they were beginning Chapter One of the Great Story which no one on earth has read: which goes on forever: in which every chapter is better than the one before."[6]

The arts bring to light what we know in our souls, deep down. We are all part of a greater story, the Story of God.

PRAYER

Gracious Father, thank you for bringing us into your story. You have made us in your image. You have made us to glorify and honor you. And though we have sinned, and have fallen into darkness, you sent us Jesus Christ. The Author of Life laid down his life to rescue us. He rose from the dead in triumph over our great enemy, death. We are now united to him by faith, and await the conclusion, your return. Develop us, Lord. Make us into the men and women you would have us be. In Jesus's name. Amen.

DISCUSSION QUESTIONS

1. What is your favorite novel, classic or modern? Why do you enjoy this story so much? Describe the characters. What tension arose that needed resolution? How is it eventually resolved?

2. What is the primary tension we see in the Story of God in the Bible? How does this tension build over the pages of the Old Testament? How is this tension resolved by Jesus Christ, particularly by his death and resurrection?

3. How do great novels typically end? How does the Story of God conclude? How does this give you hope, even in the face of trials and tragedy?

4. Great novels employ character development. How is God developing us as his people over time? How do we relate to the primary protagonist, God, as we develop?

---

6 Lewis, *Last Battle*, 228.

SPIRITUAL EXERCISES

1. Choose a classic novel which the whole congregation can read. Preach a sermon connecting the novel to God's metanarrative as laid out in Scripture. Encourage interaction within the church body over the novel.
2. Form a small group and read through a modern novel together. Get together to discuss the theological themes and practical applications of the novel which echo the great Story of God. If possible, consider using a local author and inviting him or her to come speak.
3. Write your own story in a genre of interest (historical fiction, fantasy, sci-fi, etc.) that mirrors God's Story. Make sure it includes interesting characters that develop over time, a tension that arises and finds a satisfying resolution, and a conclusion that brings it all together. Give people an opportunity to read it and offer feedback.

RESOURCES FOR FURTHER REFLECTION

1. *The Novel 100: A Ranking of the Greatest Novels of All Time* by Daniel S. Burt
2. *The Art of the Novel* by Milan Kundera
3. *On Reading Well: Finding the Good Life through Great Books* by Karen Swallow Prior
4. *Theology and Modern Literature* by Amos N. Wilder
5. *Epic: The Story God is Telling and the Role that is Yours to Play* by John Eldridge
6. *The Structure of Story: How to Write Great Stories by Focusing on What Really Matters* by Ross Hartmann

Chapter 11

Stories that Unveil
The Art of Short Story

DAVID COONS

The Parable of the Sower (1557) by Pieter Brugal the Elder

Pieter Brugel the Elder was a leader of the Flemish and Dutch Renaissance of the sixteenth century. Many of his canvases capture the beautiful vistas of his native Holland. These natural scenes are rarely ornate but are often animated with vivid depictions of everyday life. His frequent choice of common subjects earned him the nickname "Peasant Brugel."

Brugel also has an incredible talent for painting stories into these images. One of his earliest landscape paintings, *The Parable of the Sower (1557)* is its own visual parable. This beautiful yet ordinary riverscape is filled with subtle details rich in parabolic meaning. All the elements of Jesus's parable in Mark 4 have been scattered across the scene. Notice the sower, the rocky soil, the birds of the air, and even the storyteller himself. Like Jesus, the painter seems to be asking his audience, "Do you have eyes to see?"

CALL TO WORSHIP (ISAIAH 6:8–10)

Leader: Then I heard the voice of the Lord saying, "Whom shall I send? And who will go for us?"

People: And I said, "Here am I. Send me!"

Leader: He said, "Go and tell this people: '"Be ever hearing, but never understanding; be ever seeing, but never perceiving.'

People: Make the heart of this people calloused; make their ears dull and close their eyes. Otherwise they might see with their eyes, hear with their ears, understand with their hearts, and turn and be healed."

HYMN "YE SONS OF EARTH, PREPARE THE PLOUGH" BY WILLIAM COWPER (1779)

Ye sons of earth, prepare the plough,
Break up your fallow ground!
The Sower is gone forth to sow,
And scatter blessings round.

The seed that finds a stony soil
Shoots forth a hasty blade;
But ill repays the sower's toil,
Soon withered, scorched, and dead.

The thorny ground is sure to balk
All hopes of harvest there;

We find a tall and sickly stalk,
But not the fruitful ear.

The beaten path and highway side
Receive the trust in vain;
The watchful birds the spoil divide,
And pick up all the grain.

But where the Lord of grace and power
Has blessed the happy field,
How plenteous is the golden store
The deep wrought furrows yield!

Father of mercies, we have need
Of Thy preparing grace;
Let the same hand that gives me seed
Provide a fruitful place!

POEM "GOOD GROUND" BY MALCOM GUITE[1]

I love your simple story of the sower,
With all its close attention to the soil,
Its movement from the knowledge to the knower,
Its take on the tenacity of toil.

I feel the fall of seed a sower scatters,
So equally available to all,
Your story takes me straight to all that matters,
Yet understands the reasons why I fall.

Oh deepen me where I am thin and shallow,
Uproot in me the thistle and the thorn,
Keep far from me that swiftly snatching shadow,
That seizes on your seed to mock and scorn.

O break me open, Jesus, set me free,
Then find and keep your own good ground in me.

1. "Good Ground," Malcolm Guite, https://malcolmguite.wordpress.com/2015/10/10/good-ground-a-sonnet-on-the-parable-of-the-sower/. Used by permission of the poet.

SCRIPTURE READING (MARK 4:3–13, THE MESSAGE)

"'Listen. What do you make of this? A farmer planted seed. As he scattered the seed, some of it fell on the road and birds ate it. Some fell in the gravel; it sprouted quickly but didn't put down roots, so when the sun came up it withered just as quickly. Some fell in the weeds; as it came up, it was strangled among the weeds and nothing came of it. Some fell on good earth and came up with a flourish, producing a harvest exceeding his wildest dreams. Are you listening to this? Really listening?

When they were off by themselves, those who were close to him, along with the Twelve, asked about the stories. He told them, 'You've been given insight into God's kingdom—you know how it works. But to those who can't see it yet, everything comes in stories, creating readiness, nudging them toward receptive insight. These are people—Whose eyes are open but don't see a thing, Whose ears are open but don't understand a word, Who avoid making an about-face and getting forgiven.' He continued, 'Do you see how this story works? All my stories work this way.'"

THEOLOGICAL REFLECTION

If storytelling can be reckoned among the fine arts, my uncle Bob deserves recognition as one of its virtuosos. His stories aren't just woven through words; his tales are told by his whole body—facial expressions, hand gestures, varied voices, and unbridled kinetic enthusiasm. They are collected in a personal canon of narratives: *Burning Down the Basement, The Camping Trip to Prison*, and *Journeys on the Western Frontier*, just to name a few. His canon is all the more remarkable for how the details grow with each subsequent telling.

Inspired by holiday visits with my uncle, I saw my chance to become a storytelling acolyte. Gathering funny moments, family adventures, or neighborhood happenings, I became a keeper of oral tradition. During middle school, my apprenticeship found expression through creative writing. I loved the thrill of building a narrative world, elevating dramatic tension, and leading my audience into the unexpected . . . all in the span of a good story.

This internship in storytelling was an integral part of what led me into the pulpit. Today I am a storytelling preacher! While many pastors use stories as simple attention getters, or to create a quick laugh, what if pastors used stories, even in their shortest forms, to reveal truth? Could our proclamation of the gospel be strengthened by considering the work of contemporary storytellers alongside the stories that Jesus tells?

The Scriptures do not tell us much about Jesus as an artist. We have one reference, repeated in the synoptic gospels, about his handiwork as a carpenter. The New Testament is silent about Jesus the sculptor, poet, dancer, or writer. Yet, if it we consult the Gospels about Jesus the storyteller, we are given a whole portfolio of his work to ponder!

In Mark 4, we read about a whole day of storytelling that takes place along the shores of the Sea of Galilee! Jesus taught the crowd "many things by parables" (Mark 4:2). Out of all the stories Jesus told that day, Mark selects one to take center stage: "Listen, a farmer went out to sow his seed."

From the bow of a fishing boat, Jesus weaves a story about telling stories. He sows a parable about the purpose of parables. Which leaves his disciples, then and now, asking: Why does Jesus use short stories? Why, when we have audience with God in human flesh, do we get preaching in the form of parables? Why does he sneak truth in through the back door when he could more easily pound it through the front door?

Parables are Everyday Stories

The first thing I notice about Jesus's parables is their power to illustrate transcendent realities in quotidian everydayness. As Welsh commentator Matthew Henry attests, "Christ's parables are borrowed from common, ordinary things."[2] They are, quite literally, stories rooted in the soil of Palestine! Jesus prefers to couch his spiritual wisdom in vernacular that is ordinary, local, and particular.

The same could be said about the proclivities of one of America's living literary treasures, the writer Wendell Berry. Berry's interests and causes defy simple classification. He is a poet, an activist, a farmer, an environmentalist, and a localist. Some will know Berry from his articles and essays which present cultural criticism through reasoned argument and rhetoric. Yet those big ideas gain a different kind of potency when placed into the world of Berry's small-town fictions. More than fifty of Berry's short stories and numerous novels inhabit the narrative geography of a rather ordinary farm community on the Kentucky River known as Port William. Through everyday stories of hard work, harvest, war, marriage, tragedy, and friendship we enter the inner-workings of this community over more than a hundred years of its history. The pastoral quality of Berry's storytelling ensures his message is never abstracted, but always earthy, immediate, and human.

2. Quoted in Bruner, *Matthew*, 5.

For similar reasons, I think Jesus chooses parables over philosophical or spiritual propositions. Stories convey the transcendence of the kingdom of God through garden variety actors and events. They allow the Word to become flesh! Aren't we relieved that knowledge of the kingdom can be communicated not just through seminary textbooks, but in stories about the bread we bake and the birds and flowers we see?

For all the familiarity of their subject matter, however, parables may still be rather difficult to understand. Judging from the reception recounted for us here in Mark 4, parables do not always yield a harvest of understanding. More often than not, they get tangled in the weeds. So, why doesn't Jesus just tell us the truth directly?

Parables are Stories that Conceal

Ironically, Jesus chooses these everyday stories to hide in plain sight what the kingdom of God is like. There is a certain "apocalyptic" layer to the stories he tells in Galilee. Now, I realize that is not how we tend to think about parables. The "apocalyptic" genre is more often reserved for books like Revelation or Daniel, where cosmic truth is treated with cryptic imagery. Yet, what if in Jesus's more ordinary tales of God something has also been hidden?

In his book *Tell It Slant*, Eugene Peterson writes: "A parable is not an explanation... [it] does not make a thing easier; it makes is harder by requiring participation, by entering the story."[3] As Jesus makes clear in verse 9, his stories are designed for those who are really listening. His disciples must make the time to actually enter these stories. The truth of the parable can only be revealed (*apokalypsis*) to those who have "ears to hear" and "eyes to see."

Few American communities today have a resident, parable-equipped storyteller. So, where do we turn to find those gifted at hiding truth in plain sight? The closest American relation to the parable comes down to us in our short stories, through writers like James Baldwin and Ernest Hemingway. Authors who spin tales brief enough to be read in a single sitting, yet with tension enough to stay implanted in our imagination long after.

Like New Testament parables, most short stories often obscure their point before making it clear. Think of O. Henry's *The Gift of the Magi* or H.H. Munro's *The Open Window*. Both stories, now fixtures in anthologies of American literature, turn on details that we intuitively grasp have some significance but are too opaque to decipher initially. We must invest time and attention into the narrative if we are to earn the possibility of understanding.

---

3. Peterson, *Tell it Slant*, 59–60.

As we follow Jesus, something similar should be transpiring in us. Our discipleship should continually be presenting us with new details. New challenges or relationships or transitions that appear in the narratives of our lives. What has God hidden in these things that require patience and time to truly understand?

Parables are Stories that Unveil

Even as the ordinariness of parables is designed to lure us in deep enough to be troubled by what Jesus has hidden there, we should not assume that the telos of the Jesus story is to keep the audience in the dark. Parables are told in the interest of bringing us to the other side of *apokalypsis* . . . where what's hidden is finally unveiled. They are given with hope that the implanted Word of God, hidden underground for a season, will finally produce "a crop, some multiplying thirty, some sixty, some a hundred times" (Mark 4:8).

I can think of no better example of this unveiling in American fiction than the works of Flannery O'Connor. Always provocative, her stories foreground the most reprehensible aspects of our humanity. Yet even there we are reminded the Word is being sown.

One of the last stories O'Connor wrote before her death is aptly entitled "Revelation." The story begins in a doctor's waiting room where a middle-class white couple, Mr. and Mrs. Turpin, wait to be seen. As she sits, Mrs. Turpin exalts her own qualities and denigrates everyone else in town, including those sitting right there in the waiting room. She quietly surveys the others seated there—those poorer, less intelligent, and uglier than herself—and those of other races. In each case, she thanks Jesus she has not been made like one of them.

Her unfiltered pride and racism swell inside her until they are met by a violent confrontation. Mary Grace, a young college girl who becomes exasperated by the mannered hypocrisy which has surrounded her, throws her textbook at Mrs. Turpin, striking her in the head. Then, in a fit of rage she rushes across the room, wrestles Mrs. Turpin to the floor, and begins to choke the life out of her. After she is subdued and sedated, she replies to Mrs. Turpin, "What have you got to say to me? Go back to hell where you came from, you old wart hog."[4] This response strikes Mrs. Turpin with the force of another physical blow.

Looking into the eyes of her assailant, Mrs. Turpin perceives her attacker to be a messenger of divine "revelation." The rebuke issued from the lips of the angry young woman gives Mrs. Turpin "eyes to see" the grotesque

---

4 O'Connor, "Revelation," 500.

condition of her own soul. This painful unveiling eventually leads to a second transfiguring vision which arrives in final paragraphs of the story. This time what is revealed is an eschatological glimpse of true worship.

Stories are for Worship

Where are we making space for stories to renew our vision of worship? The Western paradigm for preaching is often long on explanation and analysis and short on character development, plot progression, and ironic twist. What about using stories not merely to illustrate our main ideas, but to be our primary vehicle for communication on some occasions?

A helpful precedent is practiced in synagogues every year during the reading of the *Megillot*. At prescribed times of feasting, the brevity of these five books of the Bible allow them to be read in their entirety during worship. Two of these five books, Ruth (read on Shavuot) and Esther (read on Purim), are incredible examples of biblical "short stories." The reading of the *Megillot* ushers storytelling into the liturgy.

Stories can also be a place where we learn to offer more personal expressions of worship. For most of my life, I've resigned myself to the role of an appreciator of the arts. But recently, I've realized that there is one artistic arena in my home where I exercise some artistic aptitude. I am a storyteller!

I am married to a woman who can properly claim the title "artist." She is a jeweler, a painter, knitter, and culinary artist in the kitchen. She teaches art. . . even art with preschool children! When it comes to "art," my wife Katie does it all. Almost! What I can't do with a paintbrush or a potter's wheel, I relish doing with bits of story—shading, arranging, weaving, recasting, refining and finally presenting my tales. All this, too, God receives as a beautiful act of worship!

PRAYER

As those charged with the proclamation of the Word, help us resist a gospel of mere propositions, principles, and points of application. Inspire us to inhabit Jesus's stories long enough to shape our understanding and re-tellings. Give us gospel-shaped stories that communicate your kingdom realities particular and ordinary. Show us how to hide deep truths in plain sight. May your word grow in us and take root in our souls. We pray for your stories to unveil new life in those who truly receive them.

DISCUSSION QUESTIONS

1. What are some of your favorite short stories? Why?
2. How does that particular story work? How does it communicate truth?
3. How do you feel about the idea of God "hiding" his truth?
4. What is God revealing in you right now? Is there something sprouting from a hidden place into something more visibly fruitful? Who could you share that story with?

SPIRITUAL EXERCISES

1. Choose a short narrative book in the Bible like Ruth, Jonah, or Esther. Gather a group of friends or family members to read it aloud together in one sitting. After the story is finished, take several minutes in prayer, listening and sharing the truth you received from the story. This could also be adapted to take place in a worship service.
2. Go to your local library and check out a few short story collections. Consider whether the characters or dilemmas you encounter in the pages of those stories convey any realities you know to be true of the kingdom of God. If you teach, preach, or lead worship at your church, consider how you could incorporate those stories to form a holy imagination in others.
3. Host a storytelling dinner with a group of five to ten people in someone's home. Select a theme or prompt for the night and ask each person to consider sharing a five to ten minute story on that theme. They could speak from their own experience or borrow a story they have heard somewhere else.

RESOURCES FOR FURTHER REFLECTION

1. *Tell It Slant* by Eugene Peterson
2. *The Complete Stories* by Flannery O' Connor
3. *That Distant Land* by Wendell Berry
4. *The Christian Imagination* by Leland Ryken
5. *Telling God's Story: Narrative Preaching for Christian Formation* by John W. Wright

Chapter 12

Drama Is Required
The Art of Theater

Jeff Miller

Photograph of the Bishop and Jean Valjean in the musical *Les Misérables*

In this scene from the musical, *Les Misérables*, Jean Valjean, prisoner #24601, experiences a grace that transforms the rest of his life. Famished, unable to find work, ex-convict Valjean finds mercy and food at the bishop's table but when the bishop goes to bed, he cannot resist stealing a golden candlestick he hopes will be the means to starting a new life. Immediately caught by nearby soldiers, Valjean is brought back to the bishop to face his crime. But instead of condemnation, the bishop offers Valjean the second candlestick, suggesting he forgot this part of the gift rather than betray the stealth and return him to prison—whispering to him, "I have bought your soul for God!"

CALL TO WORSHIP (I CORINTHIANS 1:21–29)

Leader: Where is the wise man? Where is the scholar? Where is the philosopher of this age? Has not God made foolish the wisdom of the world?

People: For since in the wisdom of God the world through its wisdom did not know him, God was pleased through the foolishness of what was preached to save those who believe.

Leader: Jews demand miraculous signs and Greeks look for wisdom, but we preach Christ crucified: a stumbling block to Jews and foolishness to Gentiles, but to those whom God has called, both Jews and Greeks, Christ the power of God and the wisdom of God.

People: For the foolishness of God is wiser than man's wisdom, and the weakness of God is stronger than man's strength.

Leader: Brothers, think of what you were when you were called. Not many of you were wise by human standards; not many were influential; not many were of noble birth.

People: But God chose the foolish things of the world to shame the wise; God chose the weak things of the world to shame the strong. He chose the lowly things of this world and the despised things—and the things that are not—to nullify the things that are, so that no one may boast before him.

HYMN "BUT FEW AMONG THE CARNAL WISE" BY ISAAC WATTS AND LOWELL MASON

But few among the carnal wise,
But few of noble race,
Obtain the favor of Thine eyes,
Almighty King of grace.

He takes the men of meanest name
For sons and heirs of God;
And thus He pours abundant shame
On honorable blood.

He calls the fool, and makes him know
The mysteries of His grace,
To bring aspiring wisdom low,
And all its pride abase.

Nature has all its glories lost
When brought before His throne;
No flesh shall in His presence boast,
But in the Lord alone.

SCRIPTURE READING (PHILIPPIANS 4:4–9)

Rejoice in the Lord always. I will say it again: Rejoice! Let your gentleness be evident to all. The Lord is near. Do not be anxious about anything, but in every situation, by prayer and petition, with thanksgiving, present your requests to God. And the peace of God, which transcends all understanding, will guard your hearts and your minds in Christ Jesus.

Finally, brothers and sisters, whatever is true, whatever is noble, whatever is right, whatever is pure, whatever is lovely, whatever is admirable—if anything is excellent or praiseworthy—think about such things. Whatever you have learned or received or heard from me, or seen in me—put it into practice. And the God of peace will be with you.

THEOLOGICAL REFLECTION

Besides its liveness, perhaps nothing defines theatre better than its transience. It is a house of cards. The situation is entirely crafted. The people in front of us are actors not *really* those characters. That dress is not from the eighteenth century (and those women are probably not dancing in corsets). The blood is a mix of detergent and food coloring. The gun shoots blank bullets. That poison is iced tea. That crown is made of cardboard, faux fur, and sequins. If you go through that door, you'll see lumber supports for the walls, not another room in the house. As an audience and production team, we "agree" they are a kind of "real" and then give our imaginations to that reality—to laugh, to cry, to be moved, to be provoked, ultimately, we hope, to learn about ourselves. The "is not" teaches us about the "is." The things that are not nullify the things that are.

But what, exactly, does theatre reveal? In his provocative, poignant (and, sadly, out of print) volume, *A Theological Approach to Art*, Roger Hazelton unpacks the notion that in an "unabashedly secular" world, the artist is often the one, whether explicitly or implicitly, who takes on both the priestly and prophetic task for her or his culture. Like the temple priest, the artist holds up that which is holy, good, and worthwhile for the community to reflect on, ponder, and affirm. Like a contemporary minister, the artist raises the elements we must return to, acknowledge, share, and celebrate. Like the off-putting outliers of the Old Testament, the artist as prophet calls out our wickedness, false piety, and rebellion. The prophetic artist decries that which is hollow, pretentious, cheap, and evil. Both roles are critical. Without the priest, we lose what is valuable. Without the prophet, we evade accountability.

Christians, dare I say Evangelicals, warmly embrace the priestly artist. And it's no wonder. We certainly hear plenty and see often (and know fully in our own hearts) how desperately wicked the world is. We long for an affirmation of the good, a triumph of the redemptive, a glimpse of grace. First performed in 1938, Thornton Wilder's Pulitzer Prize-winner *Our Town* is a stunning example of this. Divided into the three acts of Daily Life, Love and Marriage, Death and Eternity, the play celebrates, to borrow the words of Clyde Kilby, legendary literature professor at Wheaton College, an "awakening of amazement at the strange glory of ordinary things."[1] Usually done on a bare stage with ladders and chairs, the audience must fully conjure the everyday ordinariness of Grover's Corners with its imagination. But the absence of props and furniture underscores the transience and ineffability of the simple joys we long for—community, forgiveness, love, meaning—but often fail to see. In one of the final scenes, Emily, who has died in childbirth, is granted the opportunity to return to earth to re-experience one day of her life. She excitedly chooses her twelfth birthday but soon finds herself exasperated by all the beauty no one seems to be relishing.

> Emily: Good-bye to clocks ticking. . .and Mama's sunflowers. And food and coffee. And new-ironed dresses and hot baths. . .and sleeping and waking up. Oh, earth, you're too wonderful for anybody to realize you. She looks toward the stage

---

[1] Quoted in Piper, "God-Entranced World," https://www.crossway.org/articles/you-live-in-a-god-entranced-world/.

manager and asks abruptly, through her tears: Do any human beings ever realize life while they live it?—every, every minute?

Stage manager: 'No,' he says and pauses. 'The saints and poets, maybe—they do some.'[2]

In a recent Off-Broadway production, director David Cromer served up a sly twist in the final act in what *New York Times* theatre critic Christopher Isherwood called, "a beautiful feat of stagecraft that departs from tradition," actually revealing a working kitchen with an olfactory feast of bacon sizzling, bread baking, coffee brewing . . . simple, ordinary, everyday wonders. And in a testament to the play's enduring appeal, producer Scott Rudin, pre-Covid, announced another revival coming to Broadway in 2021, with Dustin Hoffman as the prescient stage manager.

If you prefer a musical example, you need look no further than Claude-Michel Schonberg and Alain Boublil's immensely popular *Les Misérables*, based on Victor Hugo's classic tale. Who can fail to be moved early in the musical by the bishop's surprising expression of grace when the desperate and famished Valjean is arrested, brought before him to confirm the theft of a candlestick and the bishop surprisingly insists it was a gift? Not only that, he left "the best behind," and proceeds to give Valjean more. The bishop sings:

> So monsieurs, you may release him
> For this man has spoken true
> I commend you for your duty
> May God's blessing go with you

And turning to Valjean, he confides:

> And remember this my brother
> See in this some higher plan
> You must use this precious silver
> To become an honest man
> By the witness of the martyrs
> By the passion and the blood
> God has raised you out of darkness
> I have bought your soul for God.[3]

This outrageous act of kindness leads Valjean to become a changed man. He is tested many times, to be sure, but he is fundamentally altered by grace and understands as he has been forgiven much, he needs to extend

---

2 Wilder, *Our Town*, Act III.
3 Schönberg, "Les Misérables," Act I.

that same forgiveness to others—in the end, even to his enemy. This priestly production holds up the power of grace for us to consider, embrace and, hopefully, emulate.

Christians today, like their ancient Jewish predecessors, find the prophetic artist much harder to bear, let alone engage. Again, it's understandable. Just imagine living down the street from a guy who insists on preaching naked in the streets (like Isaiah). Or a neighbor who shouts, cries, and constantly condemns your lack of faith (like Jeremiah). Or a man at your church who marries a young hooker, brings her to church in all her glory and claims he's doing it to symbolically demonstrate our own failed relationship is to God (like Hosea). That's in-your-face stuff and on top of everything else you're dealing with in your life, who needs it?

According to the Theatre Communications Group, one of the two most produced plays of 2019 was Lucas Hnath's *A Doll's House, Part 2*, an audacious exploration of what happened to Nora Helmer, the lead character of Ibsen's classic play, *A Doll's House*, after she walks out on her husband and family. The original was condemned as scandalous when it was first produced. Hnath's sequel, set fifteen years later, might be equally scandalous for some. We see Nora return to her old home, transformed by her apparent success but again living under the cloud of legal fraud because Torvald never signed the divorce papers and a judge whose wife left him, following Nora and her literary model, threatens to destroy her. Adding to Nora's discomfort, her youngest daughter is engaged to be married. And the housekeeper who raised Nora and has subsequently raised her children is angry about what she was forced to give up. And Torvald rightly asks, is it better to leave or work through difficult stuff?

In the end, the play takes no particular side. It includes conversations about relationships that could take place today. Was Nora right to leave if she felt trapped in a role that did not allow her to grow into the woman she really was? What about the kids she left behind—what has happened to them and what impact did Nora's departure have? Was Torvald really the paternalistic and condescending creature Nora cannot abide? And the nanny-housekeeper who held the family together at the expense of her own—why do we overlook those secondary characters, who are often most impacted by our actions? And why do they use those four-letter words?

One of Hnath's gifts as a writer is conflating time, helping us to see these people as not so different from us. He's also profoundly interested in spiritual issues. His widely produced earlier work, *The Christians*, explores a popular fundamental pastor's move away from traditional evangelical theology to a more inclusive, universalist doctrine. Sound familiar? But does it sound like compelling theater? In Hnath's hands, the story not only roils with real human drama, but it's told with a sparkling theatricality that is irresistible. His newer work, *Dana H*, is about a horrific experience his mother went through when Hnath was in college. Working as a chaplain in a psychiatric unit, she meets and befriends an Aryan Nation convict who has spent most of his life in jail. He abducts her and for five months, Hnath has no idea if she is dead or alive. Again, Hnath dives headlong into the spiritual messiness of this story.

A Doll's House, Part 2 exposes all the wounds and woundings of modern relationships in this frame of a sequel. Housekeeper Anne Marie finally gets to express her anger at Nora for what she did to the Helmer family as well as her own. Daughter Emmy thinks she is better equipped for life and the marriage Nora objects to precisely because of the hard knocks foisted on her by her mother's departure. Though Nora said she left the marriage because she wanted more in life, toward the end she is forced to admit to Torvald she has never found what she is looking for. Torvald says the same. The sentimentality that still infuses our ideas of intimate bonds is eviscerated. The grass is never greener on the other side. People will change, even those closest to you. And that existential longing for more that nothing fully satisfies echoes what C.S. Lewis saw as the human condition, the indication we were created for more, what only Heaven will ultimately satisfy.

That is, if you want to take the time to see and hear those plays. If you refuse because you do not agree with the theology, are threatened by the reality of darker human experience, or find yourself easily offended by raw language, you'll never engage this writer. He pulls no punches and much of what he reveals in current culture is akin to a prophetic gut punch. Who likes that? Keep your distance! Shut it down! Nearly fifty years as a theatre artist has shown me again and again that we as Christians flee the messy and confrontive. But why? We have nothing to fear. We know the truth. Unfortunately, we are uncomfortable with the sexuality, find the hint of violence unnecessary and are appalled by the words. And most of the time, the big problem is the language.

I can't tell you how many times I have received earnest admonitions about various productions I've directed that quote Philippians 4:8, "Finally, brothers, whatever is true, whatever is noble, whatever is right, whatever is pure, whatever is lovely, whatever is admirable—if anything is excellent or praiseworthy—think about such things."

I've learned to listen because, most times, the note comes from a place of genuine concern. But I've frequently been baffled by the fact that the writer—my brother or sister—takes issue with tough language but will all too quickly skim over or dismiss the greater message about racism or privilege or pride. How do we speak into "the world" unless we see it for what it is and learn to hear what's beneath the words? Are we *really offended* by language?

In his excellent book, *Imagine: A Christian Vision For the Arts*, Steve Turner makes this astute observation about Philippians 4:8:

> This verse, probably more than any other, has been used to deter Christians from the arts. It has been interpreted as meaning only look at, listen to or read things which are noble, right, pure, lovely, admirable, excellent or praiseworthy. Yet this would preclude us from passing our eyes over much of the descriptions of impurity and awfulness in the Bible. David's life would have to be read in an abridged version. Could we dwell on Job or Revelation? How could we deal with the negativity in Ecclesiastes?[4]

Please understand, I'm not saying we should make a diet of consuming everything culture offers. That would be foolish and show a lack of discernment, something we are frequently called to display. But if I can push the metaphor just a bit further, vegetables are good for you. Even the ones you don't love. Sure, some are cooked and served better than others, but a diet of sweets is not just not good for you, it's boring after a while. Being "offended" can lead to our good. When Nathan said to the King, "You are the man," David had reason to be irritated, hurt or angry and rather than turn it against the storyteller, which may have been his right, he recognized his own deep failure and repented. Paul reminds us that the gospel is an offense to those who are perishing.

Again, we should never lay aside asking God for wisdom and discernment as we approach theatre in culture today. But if we have ears to hear and eyes to see, we may be utterly astonished by unexpected reminders of his grace and truth and we may be rightfully convicted for our own pride and failures. Truth is truth. God is God. Scripture reminds us that he works through the just and the unjust. And today's theatre artists have some priestly and prophetic things to reveal on his behalf, whether they are aware of it or not!

DISCUSSION QUESTIONS

1. Think about a theater production (or moment in one) that really inspired or angered you. Why did it elicit such strong emotions? How did you process these emotions?

---

4 Turner, *Imagine*, 40.

2. Have you ever "lost yourself" while enjoying a theater production? What was the reason why you did or didn't, either way?

3. How is live theater different from watching a motion picture on a screen? How do these differences highlight the various ways God speaks to us?

4. Can you think of other artists who have performed "priestly" or "prophetic" functions in your life? Perhaps a musician, painter, or writer? How do they inspire you and hold you accountable?

SPIRITUAL EXERCISES

1. Find a community or professional play in your area that addresses important contemporary themes. Plan a trip to see it with some friends or with the youth group. Read about the play's critical themes beforehand and draft some questions to discuss together. After the play, find a location that is conducive to engage in meaningful dialogue.

2. Watch a live stream theater production as a family or group and discuss its artistic quality and any critical themes it raises. (*Hamilton* and *Les Misérables* are readily available.) Producing theaters often have educational material to assist such explorations.

3. Any portrayal of Jesus will, by definition, be limited. But what do productions like Godspell, Jesus Christ Superstar and Cotton Patch Gospel reveal about his character that we sometimes forget or overlook? How do they fall short?

4. Try reading a play together out loud using members of a class or small group. I'd highly recommend using episodes from Dorothy Sayers's *The Man Born To Be King*. Her relatively short scenes about the life of Christ are quite powerful.

5. Take a Bible story and developing it as a dramatic scene. Note the words you choose to use or not use and why. How might the entire event end differently with only a slight change?

6. If you are a preacher, craft and deliver a first-person sermon, where you preach from the perspective of a character in the Bible or in a biblical story.

RESOURCES FOR FURTHER REFLECTION

1. *The Empty Space* by Peter Brook
2. *The Empty Church* by Shannon Cragio-Snell
3. *A Theological Approach to Art* by Roger Hazelton
4. *Imagine: A Vision For Christians in the Arts* by Steve Turner
5. *Performing the Sacred: Theology and Theatre in Dialogue* by Todd E. Johnson and Dale Savidge
6. *The Performative Ground of Religion and Theater* by David V. Mason
7. *It's All in How You Tell It: Preaching First-Person Expository Messages* by Haddon and Torrey Robinson

Chapter 13

Mercy and Truth Have Met Together

The Art of Cinema

Timothy D. Bresnahan

This collage of still photographs is from Gabriel Axel's film *Babette's Feast*, which is based on Isak Dinesen's (Karen Blixen) 1958 short story of the same name. The film won the Academy Award for Best Foreign Film in 1987. It also received the BAFTA Film Award for Best Foreign Language Film. In Denmark, it won both the Bodil and Robert awards for Best Danish Film of the Year. The film was nominated for and won several other awards including a Golden Globe nomination, the Grand Prix (Belgian Film Critics Association) award and a Cannes Film Festival special prize. The film is a favorite of Pope Francis, Rowan Williams, former Archbishop of Canterbury, and renowned chef Alton Brown.

The large photograph at the top pictures the small Protestant congregation eating at Babette's feast, an exquisite seven-course French meal that she prepared to celebrate the congregation's esteemed but deceased pastor on his hundredth birthday. The elegant table is set with pressed linen, fine China, polished silver, and lit candles, which represent the presence of love. The photograph on the bottom left depicts General Lorens Lowenheilm offering a toast during dinner. The brilliant colors in his military uniform convey a stark contrast to the congregation's drab earth tones, symbolizing the general's worldly experience and ability to appreciate the finer things of life. The photograph on the bottom right shows the exhausted but satisfied look on Babette's face after the feast. She enjoys a solitary glass of wine while the carriage driver beams with delight.

CALL TO WORSHIP (PSALM 85)

Leader: Lord, You have been favorable to your land; you have brought back the captivity of Jacob.

People: You have forgiven the iniquity of your people; you have covered all their sin.

Leader: You have taken away all Your wrath; you have turned from the fierceness of your anger.

People: Restore us, O God of our salvation, And cause your anger toward us to cease.

Leader: Will you be angry with us forever? Will you prolong your anger to all generations? Will you not revive us again, that your people may rejoice in you?

People: Show us your mercy, Lord, And grant us your salvation.

Leader: I will hear what God the Lord will speak, for he will speak peace to his people and to his saints but let them not turn back to folly.

People: Surely his salvation is near to those who fear him, that glory may dwell in our land. Mercy and truth have met together; righteousness and peace have kissed.

Leader: Truth shall spring out of the earth and righteousness shall look down from heaven.

People: Yes, the Lord will give what is good; and our land will yield its increase. Righteousness will go before him and shall make his footsteps our pathway.

HYMN "LOVE EACH OTHER" BY WILLIAM J. AND LUELLA E. HENRY (1900)

Let us ever love each other
With a heart that's warm and true,
Ever doing to our brother
As to us we'd have him do.

<u>Refrain</u>
Kind and loving to each other,
Gentle words to all we meet—
Thus we follow Christ our Savior,
Proving all His service sweet.

When the heart is sad and lonely,
And the eyes with tears o'erflow,
Gentle words and deeds of kindness
Fall like sunbeams on the snow.

Let us help our fallen brother,
Lift him gently by the hand,
Speaking words of cheer and comfort,
Point him to a better land.

In this world of toil and sorrow
Many hearts are full of care;
Let us live to serve our Master,
And each other's burdens bear.

SCRIPTURE READING (JOHN 13:1–17)

It was just before the Passover Festival. Jesus knew that the hour had come for him to leave this world and go to the Father. Having loved his own who were in the world, he loved them to the end. The evening meal was in progress, and the devil had already prompted Judas, the son of Simon Iscariot, to betray Jesus. Jesus knew that the Father had put all things under his power, and that he had come from God and was returning to God; so he got up from the meal, took off his outer clothing, and wrapped a towel around his waist. After that, he poured water into a basin and began to wash his disciples's feet, drying them with the towel that was wrapped around him.

He came to Simon Peter, who said to him, "Lord, are you going to wash my feet?"

Jesus replied, "You do not realize now what I am doing, but later you will understand."

"No," said Peter, "you shall never wash my feet." Jesus answered, "Unless I wash you, you have no part with me."

"Then, Lord," Simon Peter replied, "not just my feet but my hands and my head as well!"

Jesus answered, "Those who have had a bath need only to wash their feet; their whole body is clean. And you are clean, though not every one of you." For he knew who was going to betray him, and that was why he said not everyone was clean.

When he had finished washing their feet, he put on his clothes and returned to his place. "Do you understand what I have done for you?" he asked them. "You call me 'Teacher' and 'Lord,' and rightly so, for that is what I am. Now that I, your Lord and Teacher, have washed your feet, you also should wash one another's feet. I have set you an example that you should do as I have done for you. Very truly I tell you, no servant is greater than his master, nor is a messenger greater than the one who sent him. Now that you know these things, you will be blessed if you do them.

THEOLOGICAL REFLECTION

Cinema speaks to the human condition unlike any other artistic medium. The reason for this, perhaps, is because it necessitates the collaboration of so many human beings. The production of a single motion picture combines the arts of script writing, set and costume design, producing, directing, soundtrack, musical score, special effects, camera crew, casting, acting, and the mysterious role of the key grip, who usually doesn't make an appearance until the end of the credits. All of these people pull their collective artistic talents to tell a story.

Since the dawn of motion pictures in the late nineteenth century, people have escaped into a wide array of stories showcased on the silver screen. At times, snapshots of brokenness sound an alarm that the world is not as it should be. But at other times, redemption and hope buoy the soul over portrayals of what could be. Since our Grand Director has created us to reflect his beauty and enjoy his ever-evolving story, even the art of cinema can expose glimpses of God and his kingdom. In his grace, aesthetic goodness reverberates from the screen to our hearts and minds in such a way that we are evoked to worship. Watching and reflecting on a cinematic masterpiece like *Babette's Feast* is a worshipful experience.

The film is set in a sleepy seaside village in Jutland, the remote northern peninsula of Denmark. This hamlet is the home of a conservative Lutheran sect. The founding pastor of the parish raises his two pious daughters, Martine (named after Martin Luther) and Philippa (named after Luther's friend Philip Melanchthon), in seclusion from the outside world. Martine and Philippa are physically and morally beautiful and, therefore, often catch the eye of young men in their village.

Two noteworthy men pursue the young sisters in the film. Captain Lorens Lowenheilm makes his way into the church community with the hope of winning Martine's affection, and Achille Papin, a French opera performer, takes an interest in Philippa's vocal ability. While giving Philippa voice lessons, Papin offers her his heart. But since their strict father views romance as a frivolous interruption to more pious pursuits, both sisters reject their suitors and remain unmarried. They dedicate their lives to ministering to the poor and elderly people in the village well beyond their father's passing. Martine, Philippa, and the members of their parish keep the memory of their beloved pastor alive by often quoting snippets of his sermons or reflecting on lessons he had taught them.

As the years fade into decades, few changes take place in their little town. Their banal existence is epitomized by the bland beer bread and fish soup they eat every day. But things begin to change when a strange French woman named Babette arrives on the sisters's doorstep one evening during a downpour. She is tired, soaked, and seeking refuge. She is accompanied by a letter from Achille Papin. He explains that Babette lost her husband and son in the civil war that was raging in Paris, and she has nowhere to go. In exchange for room and board, she hopes to work for the sisters as a simple servant. After a brief deliberation, the sisters grant her wish.

Babette not only left behind a luxurious life in Paris, but she also abandoned her career as the master chef at the prestigious Cafe Anglais.

Babette's existence, once marked by artistry and creativity, is now replaced by a community void of vibrancy, beauty, and life. The parish community is illuminated by the Word of God and service to "the least of these," yet there is a disconnect. The parish is plagued by a cold spirit of duty and drudgery rather than wholehearted love and joy. As the parish sings, "Jerusalem My True Home" throughout the film, they yearn for their future entrance into paradise with Christ, but they become so transfixed on the future kingdom that they fail to live fully in the present.

One day, Babette receives word from France that she has won ten thousand francs in the state lottery. She approaches Martine and Philippa and requests permission to make an elaborate French meal for the parishioners and two distinguished guests, Captain Lorens (now General Lorens) and his aunt who is the oldest member of the congregation. With hesitation, the sisters grant Babette their blessing. The feast will fall on what would have been their father's hundredth birthday. Babette not only prepares an elaborate meal, but she graciously pays for all of the exquisite ingredients.

Throughout the film, the unvarying village is captured in palettes of grey, black, and brown, but during the climactic feast, color and light burst forth. Babette's artistry warms the souls of the twelve individuals gathered at the table that night and bestows them with grace a transcendent grace that would ripple through the town with transforming power.

God the Creator crafted human beings to create—to radiate his beauty and goodness into the world—to design communities marked by life and human flourishing. In his book *Culture Care: Reconnecting with Beauty for Our Common Life*, artist and theologian, Makoto Fujimura identifies this concept as a "generative" culture. He defines generative in this way:

> At the most basic level, we call something generative if it is fruitful, originating new life or producing offspring (as with plants and animals), or producing new parts (as with stem cells). When we are generative, we draw on creativity to bring into being something fresh and life-giving.[1]

Even before the grand feast, Babette proved to be a generative figure for the village. She began to acquire fresh ingredients to prepare meals that fed the soul. She freed up the sisters so that they could better care for the flock. Babette cleaned the windows of the modest home the three women lived in to allow the light and beauty from the outside to flood in. Babette's loving presence in Jutland was *generative*. It began to impact those around her. The sisters were able to generate and save more money than ever before.

---

1. Fujimura, *Culture Care*, 22.

The food Babette prepared for the elderly in the community was crafted with care and thought and brought great encouragement.

When you watch a film like *Babette's Feast*, you can't help but ask yourself: Is my life generative? Do I lead, serve, and create in ways that breathe life in others? What gifts has God given me to glorify him and serve others? How has God blessed me to be a generative blessing to my community? Jesus of Nazareth is the perfect manifestation of what it means to be generative. He breathes life into us so we can breathe life into others.

Jesus, the Generative Giver

The hour had finally come. It was now time for the King to go to the cross to lay down his life for his sheep. It was finally time for Jesus to return to the Father and to the glory they enjoyed before the world existed (John 17:5). Jesus and the twelve were together for a meal just prior to Passover. John reminds us of the unwavering love of Christ that flowed to his followers. This was a faithful love.

Jesus was faithful to the end but one of the twelve, Judas, was being prepared by Satan to betray King Jesus. The scheme was etched upon Judas's heart and the stage was now set for the drama to unfold.

Jesus was sent from God the Father and the Father put all things under Jesus's power. Theologian D.A Carson states, "With such power and status at his disposal, we might have expected him to defeat the devil in an immediate and flashy confrontation, and to devastate Judas with an unstoppable blast of divine wrath. Instead, he washes his disciples' feet."[2] But Jesus rises from the table, and he puts on the attire of a lowly servant.

Rather than walking in the ways of a tyrant, Jesus demonstrates that true authority and power are used to serve and elevate others. He broke the common custom of the day. A rabbi or master would never wash the feet of anyone, but Jesus is different. He came not to be served but to serve and to give his life as a ransom for many (Mk 10:45). Jesus not only washes the feet of the faithful eleven, but he also washes the feet of the one that would betray him.

Likewise, Babette found herself in a community that believed in God and quoted Scripture, but Scripture did not appear to impact the hearts of the community members. They seemed to know truth, but life-giving compassion was foreign. Babette purchased the extravagant ingredients and expensive wines for the feast. She selflessly planned every detail for the

---

2. Carson, *Gospel According to John*, 462.

evening. With great humility, she placed the needs of others before her own, loving them in a tangible way that would shape all the guests for the better.

When Jesus came to Peter to wash his feet, he said to him, "Lord do you wash my feet?" Peter could not comprehend what he was witnessing. It was such a radical departure from the familiar that he could not make sense of it. It was a scandalous and incomprehensible act!

At Babette's table, the pious congregation was apprehensive about the excessive and exotic nature of the feast. Most had not experienced a fine meal like the one set before them. General Lorens, however, was quite familiar with what was taking place. Babette was preaching a profound sermon to the guests that evening without speaking a single word. The general understood the power and the beauty of the moment, and he acted as a translator so the people could comprehend what was taking place. Jesus could see that Peter was confused and so he interpreted the loving moment so that Peter and the others could understand.

"Peter, what I am doing now you do not understand, but you will later." This loving foot washing scene foreshadowed the passion to come. It is an opening act for the climactic scene to come that has our great Protagonist dying on the cross to give eternal life to all the Father had given him (John 17:2). Peter insisted that Jesus would never wash his feet. Yet Jesus responded, "If I do not wash you, you have no share with me." In other words, Peter if you do not receive the blessing of my atoning sacrifice to come, you cannot be a part of my Kingdom. You have no share in my eternal inheritance. There is no life with me or in me if you are not cleansed by my shed blood. It is at this moment we realize Jesus's loving act was pointing to something more significant. Something with eternal implications.

Upon hearing this, Peter requests a bigger bath. He did not want to miss out on being with Jesus. Jesus seems to explain that his atoning work is sufficient, that his work on the cross is a once and for all sacrifice. The eleven by faith in Jesus were seen as clean but Judas the betrayer is highlighted as the one who is not clean and therefore has no part with Jesus.

Jesus changed out of his servant's wardrobe, and he asked them if they understood what he had done. Jesus continues to illuminate the significance of the moment so the men can understand. They must understand what is happening so they can live out of that moment. Followers of Jesus are not invited to simply believe in Jesus. Followers of Jesus mimic his movements to those around them.

After the disciples watched the Messiah assume the posture of a slave to wash their feet, how could they refuse to lovingly serve those around them? How could they refuse to even love their enemies? Jesus is life-giving. His love is transformative. He is *generative* to the core. His presence beautifies and brings life. His selfless love is to be the watermark of his new community, the church. John 13:34–35 wonderfully states, "A new commandment I give to you, that you love one another: just as I have loved you, you also love one another. By this all people will know that you are my disciples, if you have love for one another."

Conclusion

The faith community in Jutland spoke of love, but their love was stale like the ghastly bread the sisters ate prior to Babette's arrival. Truth was understood and spoken but true love and mercy were tragically missing. Babette's exquisite feast was a brilliant fusion of mercy and truth commingling as movement that sparked life in the tiny village. Laughter filled the air. Authentic conversation and confession took place. Calloused souls were softened, and oneness filled the room. Toward the end of the feast, General Lorens stood to offer a toast. In his toast he further illuminated the moment, "Mercy and truth have come together. Righteousness and bliss shall kiss one another." In Christ, mercy and truth collide in transformative ways. May our lives reflect the loving service of our master!

PRAYER

Heavenly Father, thank you for your transformative love. May our lives mimic your life in such a way that tangible moments of love for those around us become the norm and not the exception. In the matchless name of Jesus, we pray. Amen.

DISCUSSION QUESTIONS

1. What are some of your favorite films? What do you like about them?
2. What aspects of the art of cinema do you appreciate most? (Plot, dialogue, acting, cinematography, etc.)
3. What film have you seen that has impacted your view of Christ?
4. Think of two people that have transformed your life with the love of Christ. What were the tangible things that they did to demonstrate his love for you?

5. As you consider your own community, how could you be a catalyst for generative change?

SPIRITUAL EXERCISES

1. Expand your film repertoire! Watch some movies that you ordinarily wouldn't watch. Explore a variety of film genres like classic, foreign, drama, historical epic, comedy, fantasy, horror, science fiction, animated, documentary, romantic comedy, sports, etc. Consider working your way through the American Film Institute's "Top 100 Films Over the Past 100 Years." Evaluate why these films are ranked so high. How do they affirm and undermine your Christian worldview?

2. Teach a theology-in-film class. Begin with a primer on basic Christian doctrine. Then watch a series of films together and discuss the theological themes. Use some of the following questions:

    a. What is this film about? What is the primary message being communicated?

    b. How does this film address issues of faith?

    c. What does this film reveal about the nature and character of God? How does it compare with what Scripture reveals about the nature and character of God?

    d. How is evil expressed in this film? How does this film portray the sinfulness and brokenness of humanity? What sins did you see?

    e. How does this film depict the doctrine of redemption? Does this film have a "Christ" figure?

    f. What types of religious symbols and images did you see? What types of religious terminology did you hear?

    g. What social or moral issues does this film deal with? What position does the film take on these issues? How does it compare with your own view?

3. Consider using movie clips, quotes, and illustrations in your church worship services and/or sermons. Teach your church community how to view films through a theological and Christological lens.

4. Invite a group of creative people in your church and community to write and produce a short film together. Once the film is created, host

a viewing party at your church. Coordinate a discussion between the writers, cast, and viewers in attendance.

RESOURCES FOR FURTHER REFLECTION

1. *Deep Focus: Theology and Film in Dialogue* by Robert K. Johnston, Craig Detweiler, and Kutter Callaway
2. *Reframing Theology and Film: New Focus for an Emerging Discipline* by Robert K. Johnston
3. *Reel Spirituality: Theology and Film in Dialogue* by Robert K. Johnston
4. *Through a Lens Darkly: Tracing Redemption in Film* by Marjorie Hewitt Suchocki
5. *A Short History of Film* by Wheeler Winston Dixon and Gwendolyn Audrey Foster

Chapter 14

The Invitation of the Table-Setting God

Culinary Art

SEAN ROBERTS

Longing for the Feast by Jocelin Yagel
Mediums: Mixed media; paint & color pencil

The Invitation of the Table-Setting God

Jocelin Yagel and her husband Tim live in Durham, Maine and attend Christ the Redeemer Presbyterian Church in Portland. As a working artist, Jocelin's illustrations frequently reference historical/religious/allegorical symbolism, and her work is informed and inspired by the illuminated manuscripts of medieval christendom Jocelin studied Fine Arts with a concentration in drawing and painting at Covenant College in Lookout Mountain, GA.

"Longing for the Feast" is an illuminated three panel timeline of God's relationship with us through food. The first panel shows creation and the garden where God gives Adam and Eve beauty all around them and fruit that is perfect and good to eat. The Hebrew word in the top left means "Begin." The second panel shows the Last Supper with Jesus at the table with his twelve disciples. The sacred elements are at the center—the bread and wine that represent what Jesus did for us and for our salvation. The third panel celebrates the modern table and what we are able to create in the kitchen because of what God has made for us to enjoy on earth. We feast today while also knowing a greater feast is still to come when we are united with God in heaven True fullness, true fulfillment, true feasting!

CALL TO WORSHIP (ISAIAH 25:1–8)

Leader: O LORD, you are my God; I will exalt you and praise your name, for in perfect faithfulness you have done marvelous things, things planned long ago.

People: You have made the city a heap of rubble, the fortified town a ruin, the foreigners' stronghold a city no more; it will never be rebuilt.

Leader: Therefore, strong peoples will honor you; cities of ruthless nations will revere you.

People: You have been a refuge for the poor, a refuge for the needy in his distress, a shelter from the storm and a shade from the heat. For the breath of the ruthless is like a storm driving against a wall and like the heat of the desert.

Leader: You silence the uproar of foreigners; as heat is reduced by the shadow of a cloud, so the song of the ruthless is stilled.

People: On this mountain the LORD Almighty will prepare a feast of rich food for all peoples, a banquet of aged wine—the best of meats and the finest of wines.

Leader: On this mountain he will destroy the shroud that enfolds all peoples, the sheet that covers all nations; the will swallow up death forever.

People: The Sovereign LORD will wipe away the tears from all faces; he will remove the disgrace of his people from all the earth. The LORD has spoken.

HYMN "THE WELCOME TABLE" (AFRICAN-AMERICAN FOLK SONG, 1874)

I'm gonna sit at the welcome table
I'm gonna sit at the welcome table one of these days, hallelujah
I'm gonna sit at the welcome table
Sit at the welcome table one of these days, one of these days

I'm gonna feast on milk and honey
Oh yes, I'm gonna feast on milk and honey one of these days, hallelujah
I'm gonna feast on milk and honey
Feast on milk and honey one of these days, one of these days

I'm gonna to tell God how you treat me
Yes, I'm gonna to tell God how you treat me one of these days, hallelujah
I'm gonna to tell God how you treat me
Tell God how you treat me one of these days, one of these days

Yes, hallelujah
Welcome table, one of these days

All God's children gonna sit together
Yes, all God's children gonna sit together one of these days, hallelujah
All God's children gonna sit together
All God's children gonna sit together, one of these days, one of these days

I'm gonna sit at the welcome table
Yes, I'm gonna sit at the welcome table one of these days, hallelujah
I'm gonna sit at the welcome table
Sit at the welcome table one of these days, one of these days
Sit at the welcome table one of these days, one of these days
Yes, gonna sit at the welcome table one of these days, one of these days

LITURGY "A LITURGY FOR THE PREPARATION OF AN ARTISANAL MEAL" BY DOUGLAS KAINE MCKELVEY (2017)[1]

Is it possible that a meal might be
so infused with a holy artistry,
so thoughtfully prepared
with intent to convey
comfort and delight,
as to make the one who consumes it
remember again,
    even for a moment,
that there is a God,
and that his care for them
    is tender?
Then let us set about
to make that meal, O Lord.
Let us ply our culinary craft
as a poet might approach her masterwork,
weighing each word and phrasing
with deliberate intention, shaping
the design as a whole,
while working nuanced echoes
of some major theme into
the finer details.
Let us thoughtfully consider
and carefully construct
the layered experience of those
who consume what we create,
so that it's pleasures and surprises
will unfold sequentially to the eyes,
the nose, the tongue, as a poem
composed of taste and texture.
Let us labor with attention paid

---

1. McKelvey, *Every Moment Holy*, 25–29.

to the tinglings of heat and spice,
to the interplay of herbs and oils,
to the minglings of things sweet and tart,
salty and sour. Let us paint in
pleasing combinations of colors
arrayed upon the plate, in complimentary
arrangements of line and form, in a
medley of aromas blending into one
bouquet. Let us play with a glad cascade
of sumptuous and savory flavors.
Let us stretch our artistry, O Lord,
using every means at our disposal,
to craft a meal that might
awaken the souls of those who share it
a yearning hunger which might only be
finally satisfied
    by the Bread of Life
    and the Wine of God,
at the time of the world's remaking.
Let us make this day a meal
that would point to that day,
a meal to remind
    of the beauty
    and the love
    and the promise
undergirding all creation.
Let us make a meal to remind
our pilgrim guests
that life will not always be so burdened,
that their days of exile will end,
that they will feast at last joyfully
in the city of their hope,
at the table of their God-King,
at the wedding feast of their Prince,
at the dawning of a golden age,

untouched by mortal sorrows.
If such a meal can be made by these hands
in this kitchen, O Lord,
then let us breathe here
the breath of your Spirit,
and let us set about
to make that meal.
Amen.

SCRIPTURE READING (SELECTIONS FROM GENESIS 1–3)

(1:27) So God created man in his own image,
in the image of God he created him;
male and female he created them.

And God blessed them. And God said to them, "Be fruitful and multiply and fill the earth and subdue it, and have dominion over the fish of the sea and over the birds of the heavens and over every living thing that moves on the earth." And God said, "Behold, I have given you every plant yielding seed that is on the face of all the earth, and every tree with seed in its fruit. You shall have them for food. And to every beast of the earth and to every bird of the heavens and to everything that creeps on the earth, everything that has the breath of life, I have given every green plant for food. . .

(2:8) And the Lord God planted a garden in Eden, in the east, and there he put the man whom he had formed. [9] And out of the ground the Lord God made to spring up every tree that is pleasant to the sight and good for food. The tree of life was in the midst of the garden, and the tree of the knowledge of good and evil.

The Lord God took the man and put him in the garden of Eden to work it and keep it. And the Lord God commanded the man, saying, "You may surely eat of every tree of the garden,[17] but of the tree of the knowledge of good and evil you shall not eat, for in the day that you eat of it you shall surely die. . ."

(3:2) And the woman said to the serpent, "We may eat of the fruit of the trees in the garden, but God said, 'You shall not eat of the fruit of the tree that is in the midst of the garden, neither shall you touch it, lest you die.'" But the serpent said to the woman, "You will not surely die. For God knows that when you eat of it your eyes will be opened, and you will be like God, knowing good and evil." So when the woman saw that the tree was good for food, and that it was a delight to the eyes, and that the tree was to be desired to make one wise, she took of its fruit and ate, and she also gave some to her husband who was with her, and he ate . . . therefore the Lord God sent him out from the garden of Eden to work the ground from which he was taken. He drove out the man, and at the east of the garden of Eden he placed the cherubim and a flaming sword that turned every way to guard the way to the tree of life. (Genesis 1:27–30; 2:8–9, 15–17; 3:2–6, 23–24)

THEOLOGICAL REFLECTION

"Are you a foodie?" This was the first question a congregant asked me and after I was called to be his new pastor. It had only been a few hours since I had arrived at my new home in Portland, Maine, and he was eagerly awaiting my answer. "Well, I really like food, but, no, I wouldn't consider myself a foodie." I immediately sensed his disappointment. But that setback soon gave way to compassion and condolence. "That's OK," he replied, "Don't worry! You will be. You can't live in Portland for long and not be!"

Portland is one of the food capitals of the country. In 2018, *Bon Appetite Magazine* named Portland it's "Restaurant City of the Year." In 2020, four of the six nominees for the James Beard Foundation's "Best Chef: Northeast" Award are in Portland or nearby towns. And it boasts more microbreweries per capita than any city in America.

Years later, I'm still not sure if I would classify myself as a "foodie," but there is no doubt that Portland has cultivated my appreciation for great food. And during my tenure, I have learned about the deep connection between our love for good food and our hunger for God. In fact, I have come to believe that the pursuit of culinary excellence is a pathway to a rich encounter with God. After all, the Bible portrays him as the "table-setting" God.

But how can masterfully crafted food call people into a relationship with the Creator? Well, I invite you to take your seat at the table and taste and see that the Lord is good. We will begin our feast with some intriguing appetizers from Genesis 1–3, then sample an array of succulent courses served throughout the scriptures, and finish with some delectable desserts from the wedding supper of the Lamb in the Book of Revelation. Who knows, maybe we'll all become foodies by the end of our feast!

A Hunger for Something Now Lost

Perhaps surprisingly, food is found on the first page the Bible. After God established the heavens and the earth and filled the sea and land with creatures, he created humanity "in his own image" and gave them dominion over all creation. But with such grand theological themes found in Genesis 1, it's easy to miss the emphasis on God's provision of food for Adam and Eve in verses 29–30:

> Then God said, "I give you every seed-bearing plant on the face of the whole earth and every tree that has fruit with seed in it. They will be yours for food. And to all the beasts of the earth and all the birds of the air and all the creatures that move on the ground— everything that has the breath of life in it— I give every green plant for food." And it was so.

Notice how God's first known words to human beings are centered on food. His culinary provision teaches us some important truths.

First, humans beings were created as people who hunger. This is significant for several reasons, but most importantly, because it shows us that we are not self-contained, self-sustained, autonomous creatures. Instead, we were created dependent on something else for life. Orthodox priest Alexander Schmemann makes the point that the world is presented as "an all-embracing banquet table for man, [and food] the central image of life."[2]

In addition to the fact that we were created hungry, we learn that our hunger introduces us to God as the one who feeds and fills. Food, therefore, was never meant to be an end in itself, but comes to us as an invitation to him, as the One who ultimately satisfies our deepest hungers and longings. And it comes, not as something earned, but as a gift of his grace. It may be difficult for modern people to see, but the author of Genesis is making a radical claim about the nature of God's generosity. In the context of the Ancient Near East, there is no precedent or parallel for this. In every other creation account, gods create humans to feed them. But here in Genesis, God sets a table for humanity—as an expression of his amazing grace, tender care, and steadfast love. It's incredible!

But as you flip the page to Genesis 2, God's skill as the Divine Culinary Artist is on display even more clearly the Garden of Eden. The author of Genesis describes the beauty and abundance in verses 8–9: "And the Lord God planted a garden in Eden, in the east, and there he put the man whom he had formed. And out of the ground the Lord God made to spring up every tree that is pleasant to the sight and good for food."

---

2. Schmemann, *Life of the World*, 17.

The author uses gardening verbs to highlight God's special care and attention to detail. God's artistic genius is exhibited in each tree and fruit, with its unique color, texture, aroma, and flavor. God is the divine gardener who produces the amazing array of food for the "garden to table" feast that he has prepared for Adam and Eve.

Notice too, the emphasis on beauty. There is a deep connection between that which is "pleasant to the sight" and that which is "good for food." In fact, when Eve eats the forbidden fruit, she is largely motivated by its aesthetic beauty. God showcases his affection for Adam and Eve by creating food that is pleasing to both the eye and the tongue. Theologian Norman Wirzba observes, "Food is God's love made nutritious and delicious given for the good of each other."[3] Likewise, Schmemann, notes:

> In the Bible, the food that man eats, the world of which he must partake in order to live . . . All that exists is God's gift to man, and it all exists to make God known to man, to make man's life communion with God. It is divine love made food, made life for man . . . Behind all the hunger of our life is God.[4]

From the beginning, God has set the table and provided an appetizing meal for us to savor the greatest truth that our hunger reveals. In all of these things, God expresses his deep desire for communion with us. We know from our own experience that eating and drinking together creates the context for relationship. Our tables are platforms for meaning and intimacy. If we want to get to know someone, our most natural way is an invitation "out to dinner" or "to grab a beer" (or a cup of coffee) or "to come over for a meal." It's why when we throw a party, or have a celebration, or observe a holiday, it often revolves around the act of eating.

There is something mysterious about a meal's ability to forge friendships, deepen intimacy, and create community. God created human beings with the capacity and desire to eat and drink and enjoy communion with him and others. He also provided everything necessary to fulfill these capacities and desires. Since food provided one of the original pathways to a relationship with God, could it not also impart an invitation for humanity to reenter communion with the One who made us?

---

3. Wirzba, *Food and Faith*, xii.
4. Schmemann, *Life of the World*, 21.

A Table Now Being Prepared

It is within this theological framework that we can better apprehend the tragedy of the fall in Genesis 3. Out of the abundance and beauty of the Garden, God gave one command: "You may surely eat of every tree of the garden, but of the tree of the knowledge of good and evil you shall not eat, for in the day that you eat of it you shall surely die" (Gen 2:16–17). This command reinforces the idea that eating in the Garden takes place in the context of a relationship of faith and trust with God. It is, therefore, not coincidental that the serpent uses food as his primary means of temptation. If food fosters communion with God, then the strategy of the Deceiver is most effective if he appeals to humanity's eating habits. Thus, we could say, the fall happens as the result of an "eating disorder." Adam and Eve are deceived into believing that they can satisfy their hunger apart from communion with God.

The result was devastating. When Adam and Eve ate the forbidden fruit, communion with God was broken—and now we find that our once good hunger devolves into insatiable appetites. We see evidence of it all over the world and in our own lives. Our world is filled with people hungering after things that cannot satisfy—relationships, sex, money, power, success, prestige, politics, affirmation, activistic pursuits, experiences, romance, substances, knowledge, stuff—the list is endless. Of course, these things are not bad in and of themselves, but any one of them can lose their proper place in our life when consumed in an attempt to fill that which was lost. This is true even of food itself—we have long forgotten that it was meant to point us to something even greater.

It's no surprise, then, that from this point forward, many key themes in the Bible involve hunger. What was once a world of abundance is now a world of scarcity. For instance, even the Book of Genesis, which began in a garden of abundance, ends with a worldwide famine. Throughout the rest of the Pentateuch Israel is wandering around the desert looking for food. The Psalmist and the Prophets will later speak of striving, in the words of Isaiah, "for that which does not satisfy" (Isa 55:2). And from a Christian perspective, we see humanity inescapably stuck in a misguided attempt to return to that feast we forfeited.

However, there is good news! The amazing truth of the gospel is that in this world of scarcity, God remains a God who abundantly provides. As the Old Testament unfolds, God uses detailed and carefully prepared meals as a context for restoring people to himself. We see this in his choosing of Israel. What began as a makeshift meal between God and Abraham at the great oaks of Mamre (Gen 18)[5] would later be formally instituted as a Passover meal (Exod 11). This theme would be reiterated through God's constant provision in the wilderness (Exod 16, Num 11), codified into the Law (Lev 23), embodied in the fertility of the Promised Land (Exod 3, Num 13), liturgized in the Psalms (Ps 104), foretold in the prophets (Isa 25:55), and lamented in the exile (Lam 1:4).

Eventually, this theme of God providing abundance amidst scarcity would crescendo at that wonderful moment when a young virgin, upon finding she is pregnant, sang a praise song to the God who, in the conception of her Messiah/Son, once again "filled the hungry with good things" (Luke 1:53). It's no surprise that one author summarizes the whole story of Israel as, "They tried to kill us. We survived. Let's eat!" He goes on to say that that narrative, now transformed in the work of Christ enables a new motivation for eating: "I love you! I forgive you! Let's eat!"[6]

An Invitation Awaiting Response

It is not coincidental that Jesus began his ministry by going into the wilderness to fast. In the Incarnate Son, we see the God of the universe entering into the scarcity and hunger that is so prevalent in the world. And yet, this picture of Jesus's scarcity is balanced by abundance—Jesus brought renewed feasting. We see this in his first miracle of changing water into wine at the wedding feast in Cana of Galilee (John 2) and his multiple miraculous mass feedings (Matt 14 and 15). We see it in the criticisms that the religious leaders leveled against him: "Look at him! A glutton and a drunkard, a friend of tax collectors and sinners!" (Luke 7:34) and in his responses to those criticisms: "How can the guests of the bridegroom fast while he is with them? They cannot, so long as they have him with them" (Mark 2:19).

In fact, feasting is a controlling metaphor in Jesus's teaching about the nature of the kingdom. For instance, in the preface to his parable of the Great Banquet, Jesus says, "Blessed is the man who will eat at the feast in the kingdom of God." (Luke 14:15) And in perhaps the greatest example of scarcity or abundance in the gospels, the prodigal son's longing to fill his stomach with the pods the pigs were eating is transformed into the provision of a fatted calf as the main course of the celebration feast in Jesus's supreme parable. Jesus embodies the "Good News" of the kingdom by inviting "sinners" to sit with him at his table and join in the feast.

---

5. See also 2 Chron 20:7, Isa 41:8, James 2:23.
6. Sweet, *Tablet to Table*, 5.

The Invitation of the Table-Setting God 155

Therefore, the possibility for renewed communion is expressed at each meal shared, and with each sinner engaged. But it's not until the Last Supper that this possibility is fully displayed. Here is where we find the true meaning of Jesus's once cryptic claim that he himself is "The Bread of Life" who "comes down from heaven to give life to the world" (John 6). And here at this table, we see the full cost of our restored communion. For us to feast, Jesus now must fast (Luke 22:15–17). For us to sit at the table again, Jesus must thirst on the cross. The bread of life must be broken, and his blood must be shed for "the forgiveness of sin" (Matt 28:28). For us to find the food that ultimately satisfies our hunger, Jesus must die a sacrificial, substitutionary, and atoning death on our behalf.

And yet, I'm always struck by the modesty of this table. All the great feasts of the Old Testament are elaborate, but the elements of this table are simple—bread and wine. The feast in the Garden and the feast at the end of time are both lavish, but this table is ordinary and mundane. Bread represents necessity and sustenance. Wine is a symbol of blessing and joy. It's as if these elements are chosen simply as a frame so as not to detract from the true beauty of this feast. Jesus is the true "culinary masterpiece" for which our hungry souls long. In the simplicity of bread and wine, we see him as the sustenance our soul needs and our truest delight. Food was never meant as an end in itself—it was always meant to invite us into something greater.

From the church's earliest days, Christians have been uniquely shaped by tables (Acts 2:42–47). It was around tables that Christians encouraged one another, were known by one another, and lived life with one another. And it was through shared meals at tables that they invited their neighbors to "taste and see" the goodness of the Lord and the kingdom abundance he had brought through his Son.

Jesus's table shaped the common table of their gathered worship and the scattered tables of their hospitable homes. His table enabled them to look toward the table of their promised hope at the wedding supper of the Lamb on the last day. There is no table in our human experience that better expresses the height, depth, and breadth of intimacy and communion than a wedding table. It is unsurpassed! Thus, Scripture ends with God welcoming humanity to the great banquet table to celebrate the consummation of human history where Creator and creation is fully restored, and heaven and earth become one once again. And there, in a world in which, "all things are made new," we will feast forevermore.

Thus, with this image–a full table with all the sights and smells and sounds and flavors we might imagine—Scripture finds its natural conclusion. But in case, somehow, in the long stretch from Genesis to Revelation you somehow missed it, the final chapters of the Bible extend an invitation- for you to join the feast.

> "Blessed are those who are invited to the wedding supper of the lamb!... The Spirit and the Bride say, "Come" (Rev 19:9, 22:17).

Pondering the Potential

Now that we have sampled the story of culinary art throughout Scripture, I want to challenge you to think about the possibilities of culinary art in your own context. Think about the stories of people who have built their lives around good food—the barista who carefully crafts two cups of cappuccino for a conversation shared between old friends; the chef whose cauliflower dish (yes, cauliflower!) might one day win him a James Beard Award; the sommelier whose palette can express the complexities of a fine glass of Pinot Noir; and the baker who displays a masterful queue of breads and confections in his store-front window. I wonder if this insatiable drive to create the consummate bite and find the perfect sip just might be a small manifestation of the hunger for that which was lost—an unknown desire for a table now set, and the subtle yearning for communion with our table-setting God.

Perhaps this invitation is not just for our world, but also for the church. It's easy for Christians to live lives that never realize that we are recipients of an abundant gourmet feast. Ponder the potential for the Christian church to respond to God's culinary invitation anew! Ponder the potential for the church to develop and deepen its communion with God and each other in community through a renewed commitment to feasting! Ponder the potential for local churches to herald Christ's kingdom through a renewed appreciation of culinary art!

Conclusion

In her brilliant short story "Babette's Feast," author Karen Blixen ignites our imaginations to this potential. In the climactic scene, Babette, a French housekeeper, prepares a lavish meal for a small stoic congregation despite their skepticism and resistance. But as the little flock eats the meal together, the community begins to change. Laughter renews old friendships. Long-strained relationships are healed. And flavorful food opens their hearts to joyful tears of repentance. In Blixen's words,

The rooms had been filled with a heavenly light . . . Taciturn old people received the gift of tongues; ears that for years had almost been deaf were opened to it. Time itself had merged into eternity. Long after midnight the windows of the house shone like gold, and golden song flowed out into the dark.

But then she says this:

"When later in life they thought of this evening it never occurred to any of them that they might have been exalted by their own merit. They realized that . . . infinite grace . . . had been allotted to them, and they did not even wonder at the fact, for it had been the fulfillment of an ever-present hope. The vain illusions of this earth had dissolved before their eyes like smoke, and they had seen the universe as it really is. They had been given one hour of the millennium . . . Their hearts suddenly filled with gratitude.[7]

Culinary art has a unique way of demonstrating the lavishness of God's grace as he "sets a table before us" and lovingly invites us into relationship with himself. May we all taste that grace by responding to the culinary invitation of our table-setting God.

PRAYER

Gracious Father, may this be our prayer: that we might taste your grace and respond to your culinary invitation. We thank you that you created us hungry and gave us all the joys of food—with its smells, colors, textures, and tastes. And we are grateful for this incredible invitation into relationship with you.

Help us to ward off the temptation to fill our hungers and longings outside of communion with you. And bring us once again to your table of grace—that in feasting and fellowship with you and your people we might be filled anew with your abundant love.

May your table shape all the other tables at which we eat—that through good food and good drink we might extend your culinary invitation to a world desperate for you. And may we do it with beauty, artistry, and lavish, self-sacrificial generosity—that we might experience a foretaste of the Wedding Feast to come! We pray this in the name of our table-setting Savior, Jesus Christ our Lord. Amen.

---

7. Dinesen, *Anecdotes of Destiny*, 53–54, 55.

DISCUSSION QUESTIONS

1. Describe one of the best meals you've ever experienced! Can you recall a time when a meal spiritually moved you? Has a meal ever affected your faith?
2. How might culinary art express God's relational invitation to a hungry world?
3. How does our communion table at church shape our own family tables? How could our tables be more welcoming of our neighbors?
4. What are some ways this has encouraged you to engage in culinary art—either through eating and experiencing, or preparing and cooking?

SPIRITUAL EXERCISES

1. *Eating:* Eat good food and attempt to cook great meals with tables full of neighbors, family, and friends.
2. *Cooking:* Consider learning how to cook foods outside of your normal repertoire, especially exploring new culinary worlds. Purchase a cookbook that teaches you how to cook cuisine from another culture and give it a try.
3. *Exploring:* Visit local restaurants and enter into diverse and/or multi-ethnic culinary worlds. Ask to meet the chef and thank the restaurant staff for the way they serve through food.
4. *Connecting:* Contemplate how food might be a pathway for you to build deeper relationships with people in your local community (take a cooking class, visit the same breweries or restaurants and get to know the people who work there, prioritize attending special food events and festivals, etc.)
5. *Praying:* Practice mindful preparation and eating. As you do so, pray prayers of thanksgiving for the way God uses food to communicate his love to you. Use a Psalm, Scripture reading, liturgy, or a written prayer about food.
6. *Hospitality:* Practice hospitality with food in your home. Experiment with how food can be used to network Christian friends with neighbors and other friends or family who may not be Christians. Coordinate

a culinary gathering for your Christian community (i.e. community groups, bible studies, informal gatherings, etc.). Include those who may not have access to good food and discuss the experience.

RESOURCES FOR FURTHER REFLECTION

1. *Echoes of Eden: Reflections on Christianity, Literature, and the Arts* by Jerram Barrs
2. *Created & Creating: A Biblical Theology of Culture* by William Edgar
3. *The Supper of the Lamb: A Culinary Reflection* by Robert Farrar Capon
4. *Babette's Feast and Other Stories* by Isak Dinesen (Karen Blixen)
5. *Food: A Very Short Introduction* by John Krebs
6. *Food and Faith: A Theology of Eating* by Norman Wirzba

Chapter 15

The Great Vintner
The Art of Winemaking

BRIAN BETHKE

The Wedding Feast at Cana (1819) by Julius Schnorr von Carolsfeld

The Great Vintner

Julius Schnorr von Carolsfeld (1794–1872) was a German Lutheran painter. Early in his career, he associated with the painters of the Nazarene movement who sought a revival of Renaissance style in religious art. He is remembered for his extensive Picture Bible, and his designs for stained glass windows in cathedrals throughout Europe.

In his painting *The Wedding Feast at Cana*, Carolsfeld pictures the wedding celebration as an elaborate outdoor banquet. The newlywed couple is sitting together on the right under a rounded trellis covered lightly with greenery. They are sitting in the place of honor. Mary is standing behind Jesus, advocating for his intervention. Jesus is in the foreground, directing the servants. His first miracle of changing water into wine is the center of attention. In the background, the wedding is in full swing with many guests at the banquet. There is music, food, and drinking.

CALL TO WORSHIP (AMOS 9:11–15)

Leader: "In that day I will restore David's fallen tent. I will repair its broken places, restore its ruins, and build it as it used to be, so that they may possess the remnant of Edom and all the nations that bear my name," declares the LORD, who will do these things.

People: "The days are coming," declares the LORD, "when the reaper will be overtaken by the plowman and the planter by the one treading grapes. New wine will drip from the mountains and flow from all the hills.

Leader: I will bring back my exiled people Israel; they will rebuild the ruined cities and live in them. They will plant vineyards and drink their wine; they will make gardens and eat their fruit.

People: I will plant Israel in their own land, never again to be uprooted from the land I have given them," says the LORD your God.

HYMN "O CHRIST, THE KING OF HUMAN LIFE" BY GEORGE H. BOURNE (1867).

Bourne wrote this hymn for his sister's wedding. She married Allan Webb, the future Bishop of Bloemfontein, South Africa.

O Christ, the King of human life,
In royal bounty pour
On these Thy servants, man and wife,
Thy blessing evermore.

On ties of home, in life, in death,
Thy seal divine was set:
Those thirty years at Nazareth
Thou, Lord, rememberest yet!

And by these holy years, we pray,
To these Thine own be nigh:
Their common life from day to day
Direct and sanctify.

At Cana's marriage first didst Thou
Thy glory manifest;
Oh, come to be among us now
A wonder-working Guest!

Poor weakly elements are ours,
But wealth and might are Thine:
Rule earthly life by heavenly powers,
The water change to wine!

And in Thy faith, and in Thy fear,
May these united be,
True type of those espousals dear
Between Thy Church and Thee.

So let them both at last attain
That better country's coast,
Where with the Father Thou dost reign
And with the Holy Ghost.

SCRIPTURE READING (JOHN 2:1–12)

On the third day there was a wedding at Cana in Galilee, and the mother of Jesus was there. Jesus also was invited to the wedding with his disciples. When the wine ran out, the mother of Jesus said to him, "They have no wine."

And Jesus said to her, "Woman, what does this have to do with me? My hour has not yet come."

His mother said to the servants, "Do whatever he tells you."

Now there were six stone water jars there for the Jewish rites of purification, each holding twenty or thirty gallons.

Jesus said to the servants, "Fill the jars with water." And they filled them up to the brim.

And he said to them, "Now draw some out and take it to the master of the feast."

So they took it. When the master of the feast tasted the water now become wine, and did not know where it came from (though the servants who had drawn the water knew), the master of the feast called the bridegroom and said to him, "Everyone serves the good wine first, and when people have drunk freely, then the poor wine. But you have kept the good wine until now."

This, the first of his signs, Jesus did at Cana in Galilee, and manifested his glory. And his disciples believed in him. After this he went down to Capernaum, with his mother and his brothers and his disciples, and they stayed there for a few days.

THEOLOGICAL REFLECTION

Years ago, my wife Erica and I were celebrating our wedding anniversary in the central California coast wine region. The landscape was breathtakingly beautiful: filled with rolling green hills, endless rows of exotic grape vines, and perfect spring weather. Vineyards were scattered abundantly as various vintners invited wine region pilgrims to experience the fruits of their labor, literally. As amateur wine connoisseurs, the goal of our pilgrimage was to taste the best the region had to offer. With each winery visit, we asked the local sommelier (wine steward) for a recommendation that would direct the next step in our journey. One of the recommendations we received was a place called *Demetria*.

Demetria was not on the list of wineries we received from our hotel. We were told by the sommelier that we would have to call ahead and make an appointment. We called and were given an obscure address and vague directions. We entered the destination in our GPS and resumed our quest. We soon discovered that Demetria was off the main path and situated in the remote hills of Los Olivos, California. At one point, we ended up on a dirt road, pressed in by rows of grape vines on both sides. On the verge of feeling lost and giving up, the road opened up to reveal a beautiful Greek-style villa. A solitary gentleman stood outside. The warm smile and eager excitement on his face told us that he could not wait to share something with us. He welcomed us as if we were long-time friends, even perhaps family. Then he sat down, poured us some wine, and motioned for us to taste.

As I sampled the 100% Syrah varietal, I could taste the creative complexity and uniqueness brought about by the central coastal fog and Los Olivos soil. As I savored the artisanal mastery of this wine the words of the Benedictine monk, Dom Perignon, when tasting his wine for the first time, echoed through my mind, "Come quickly, I'm drinking the stars!" There was something soulfully intoxicating about that moment. Something which felt victorious in some cosmic way. I immediately knew this was no ordinary wine and this was no ordinary moment. It was a foretaste of something eternal to come. It was transformative. It was, dare I say, a sacramental moment. Seeing the pleasure on our faces, the gentleman introduced himself as Alexis. He was the Vintner.

Have you ever had a moment similar to mine? Have you ever experienced something, maybe as simple as a glass of wine, that seems to point to something bigger, something transcendent? It almost sounds sacrilegious to say. Thankfully, John chapter 2 helps us process these questions as we are introduced to another vintner, "The Great Vintner," our Lord Jesus Christ, who transforms everything.

Jesus is the Great Vintner Who Transforms History

As Jesus began his earthly ministry in Galilee, we soon learn that he was invited to a wedding at Cana. Wedding feasts were major events in near eastern culture and lasted up to seven days. The host would invite as many people as possible to celebrate this joyous occasion. A main staple in the celebration was wine. Throughout the Old Testament, abundance and blessing were described in terms of fruit from the vine. Wine was not needed for daily substance, but it was reserved for special occasions, usually celebrations of joy.

Therefore, wine, the pinnacle product of the fruit from the vine, from a Jewish context, represented God's abundant blessing for enjoyment. Guests would drink wine and enjoy one another for seven days. It was expected that the host and bridegroom would provide enough wine for all seven days. It is in the midst of these festivities we find our Lord Jesus Christ enjoying wine, people, and celebrating the marital union of a man and woman.

We soon discover things are not well. Mary, Jesus's mother somehow receives word that the wine has ran out. The women's quarter was often near where wine was stored. It is likely then that Mary hears the news before Jesus. Running out of wine in the midst of a wedding would have been socially disastrous, a subject of ridicule for years. She knows a miracle is needed or the family history of these newlyweds and their extended family will be tainted forever. She goes to the only person who could do anything about it, the one she trusts will respond, Jesus.

At first glance, Jesus responds strangely, even rudely to his mother as he addresses her as "Woman." However, culturally this was an equivalent of calling your mother "Ma'am." Not exactly warm, he was establishing a polite distance from Mary. He tells her that his "hour," a veiled reference to the cross, had not yet come. But with unflappable faith, Mary knows her son, the Son of God, the Great Vintner, will do something and tells the servants to accommodate whatever request he asks of them.

In the 1987 Danish drama *Babette's Feast*, the puritanical, stoic guests arrive at the great feast harboring years of relational wounds. However, as they taste the multiple wines the atmosphere is changed. They talk, enjoy one another. Wounds are healed, transformation takes place, history is changed. It was not an ordinary feast. The feast at Cana was no ordinary wedding feast and Jesus was no ordinary guest.

The wine, which represent God's blessing had run dry. Hope was lost. Disaster was imminent. A transformative Messianic bridegroom who would provide a free-flowing fount of wine for a joyful eternal banquet was needed. The good news is that Jesus responds! This moment started the clock towards the "hour" that Jesus, the Great Vintner would be crushed in the divine winepress and provide the wine of himself so we could avoid disaster, have everlasting hope, and celebrate relational Trinitarian love forever. This moment changed every facet of human experience and history!

Here is the real question, the personal question—has it changed your history? Has it changed your human experience?

Jesus is The Great Vintner Who Transforms the Old into New

I could imagine at this point guests are seeing some anxious bustling from the host and servers. Perhaps, people are wondering why their wine glasses have not been filled. I am sure the master of the feast, which was an honorific position, could feel the glare of guests who were wondering why he was slacking on the job. In the midst of this tension Jesus tells the servants to fill six stone thirty-gallon jars with water. These were not ordinary jars. These were purification jars used to ceremonial cleanse. These jars represented the Jewish religious and sociological liturgy. Using these jars for anything other than for a socio-religious purposed would defile them.

Imagine being one of the servants. Filling those jars would have taken awhile. The whole time wondering, "What is going on here?" or "This makes no sense!" Jesus showing more concern for the bride and bridegroom than for contemporary rituals ensures the jars get filled. The master of the feast, probably at the point of a nervous breakdown, tastes the liquid in the six jars which has now been transformed to wine. Bewilderment to the origin of the wine gives way to pragmatism as he calls the bridegroom over for a quick update. This wine is bound to transform the entire place!

Author and theologian Gisela H. Kreglinger grew up on a family vineyard in the Rhone Valley. In her book *The Spirituality of Wine* she describes the active nature of wine: "Wine is 'alive' in the sense that it continues to evolve even after it has been bottled, and thus it is not a static object. When vintners speak about wine having a 'soul', they are hinting at this capacity of wine to evolve and mature over time."[1]

In this first recorded miracle, we see Jesus's re-creative power. His eschatological purposes are on display. Through this miracle, he declares that the old order of things is no more; the Messianic Age and his kingdom is now upon us. The Great Vintner takes non-living water and transforms it into active, soulful wine. He is declaring that he is making all things new until it reaches full maturity upon his return and eternal shalom is a normative reality. As his kingdom people, the one invited to his marriage supper, he is calling us to participate in his re-creative effort. He longs to change every place and space of the entirety of creation. After all, it is his! This means that your work, even the smallest task, your acts of love towards others, even seemingly most insignificant, matter to him. He will use it towards his recreative purpose. The old is becoming new!

It was not an accident that Jesus found himself in Cana and around those specific people to display this recreative miracle. So, it is with every one of us, it is not an accident we are where we are at surrounded by those we are around. The questions before us all, before you, have to be: Where does recreation need to happen in your everyday life? Who is he calling you to bring the new wine of the kingdom?

Jesus is The Great Vintner who Transforms the Ordinary to the Extraordinary

If you are even an amateur wine connoisseur, the million-dollar question on your mind has to be, "What did the wine taste like?" Although the biblical account doesn't give us tasting notes, we know it was good! The master of the feast seems to almost reprimand the bridegroom for breaking protocol by serving the poor wine first and serving the good wine last. This reprimand

---

1. Kreglinger, *Spirituality of Wine*, 15.

The Great Vintner

would surely be motivated by the wine being exquisite. Good can mean a lot of things but the master of the feast must have recognized the regional uniqueness of the wine yet on a magnified level. This wine represented an immanent familiarity and yet, a transcendent mystery. It was clear that Jesus's wine was superior to all other wines.

In this act, Jesus challenges our whole thinking on the connection between the secular and sacred, the profane and sanctified, the ordinary and extraordinary. In our western thought, we have been so influenced by a philosophical dualism that bifurcates the physical and the spiritual connectiveness. Here, through wine, good wine, superior wine, the Great Vintner Jesus destroys that divide as he communicates a spiritual reality through a physical, and may I add, the enjoyable gift of wine.

Again, Krenglinger provides interesting insight specifically as it relates to the Holy Eucharist and the spiritual aspect of everyday things when she states,

> The Lord's Supper further challenges dualistic understanding of spirituality. In the Lord's Supper we embrace, cherish, and practice the God-given interconnectedness between spiritual and material realities; we learn to see the extraordinary in the ordinary. The use of seemingly ordinary things, such as bread and wine, in the Lord's Supper challenges us to see everyday aspects of our lives are imbued with spiritual meaning.[2]

What does this mean? Simply, it means Jesus makes everything better! He is what makes the ordinary things of life extraordinary. He is what transforms an everyday, ordinary moment to an extraordinary, sacramental moment. In a practical sense, when we enjoy his creative abundance with an understanding that it is a gift from him, we bring him glory! The whole point of this miracle was so that Jesus could manifest his glory. In some mysterious way, when we enjoy the ordinary with christocentric lenses, we bring him glory and the thin space between heaven and earth comes even closer.

Conclusion

As I reflect on that experience at Demetria with my wife Erica, Alexis the vintner, and the wine, I realize it was a moment when Jesus, The Great Vintner, revealed his Messianic character. He peeled back a layer of this reality and revealed the reality of what is to come. It was transformative. The disciples had the same experience. In fact, John tells us that in response to this miracle "his disciples believed him." They were transformed.

---

2. Kreglinger, *Spirituality of Wine*, 2.

You see, vintners transform things. They take grapes from a particular place and time and craft them in a way that maintains the elements of the grape but transform them into a whole new active element and experience. Jesus is doing this now and he longs to transform your life, your place, everything. Will you experience his wine? Will you believe him?

Do you desire to bring our Great Vintner glory and experience him in a deeper way? Stop and enjoy him through the ordinary things of life. Perhaps start by enjoying a glass of good wine with good friends. Cheers!

PRAYER (A LITURGY FOR ENJOYING NEW WINE WITH FRIENDS)[3]

A new bottle of wine will be poured into glasses and given to each participant. All participants will take a moment to move it around their glass to notice the visual characteristics and beauty of the wine.

Celebrant: To gather joyfully is indeed a serious affair, for drinking new wine and all enjoyments gratefully taken are, at their heart, acts of war.

People: In celebrating this gathering around good wine we declare that evil and death, suffering and loss, sorrow and tears, will not have the final word.

All participants will take a moment to enjoy the aroma of their wine and take note of the aromatic pleasures of the wine.

Celebrant: But the joy of fellowship, and the welcome and comfort of friends new and old, and the celebration of these blessings of new wine and conversation and laughter are true evidences of things eternal, echoes of the great celebration that awaits the Bride of Christ, and are the first fruits of that great glad joy that is come and that will be unending.

People: So, let our gathering this day be joined to those sure victories secured by Christ.

Celebrant: Let it be to us now a delight, and a glad foretaste of his eternal kingdom.

All participants will slowly taste their wine, enjoying and engaging their senses. After a moment of reflection, all participants will then lift their glasses.

All: Blessed are You O Lord our God. King of the universe who creates the fruit of the vine.

Celebrant: And, "Blessed are those who are invited to the marriage supper of the Lamb."

All: Amen! Alleluia, Alleluia, Alleluia!

---

[3] Adapted from McKelvey, *Every Moment Holy,* 112–115.

DISCUSSION QUESTIONS

1. What is your favorite type of wine? What draws you to this particular type?
2. In what practical ways does the idea of "re-creation" challenge your view of heaven and earth?
3. How do you see the divide between secular and sacred manifest in your life?
4. Why is the concept of having "sacramental moments" important for human flourishing in a post-Christian context?

SPIRITUAL EXERCISES

1. Pour a glass of your favorite wine and find a quiet place to relax. This can be a place indoors or outdoors. Read John 2:1–12 slowly, three times. Engage your biblical imagination and try and put yourself in the story. What do you see? What do you smell? What do you hear? From what or whose perspective are you finding yourself identifying with? As you ponder these questions, take sips of your wine, paying special attention to how you feel, listening to the Holy Spirit. What is the Holy Spirit saying to you through this exercise?
2. Pour a glass of wine for one extra person (example: if you are by yourself, pour two glasses; if there are two people, pour three glasses). Read Amos 9:14–15 and John 2:1–12. Imagine Jesus joined you at your table. He is sitting with you, drinking wine and enjoying your company. What do you want to say to him? Have a prayerful conversation with him, as if he was physically there (all participants). If you are not alone, process this conversation with one another over another glass of wine. Feel free to engage Jesus again!
3. Host a dinner party. Invite friends to each bring a bottle of wine. Open the event with a celebratory tasting using the above "A Liturgy For Enjoying New Wine with Friends." Ask each person to taste and describe the wine and what thoughts, emotions, memories it evokes. Offer brief prayers of thanks, through a toast, after each round.

RESOURCES FOR FURTHER REFLECTION

1. *The Spirituality of Wine* by Gisela H. Kreglinger
2. *Every Moment Holy* by Douglas Kaine McKelvey
3. *Liturgy of the Ordinary* by Tish Harrison Warren
4. *Wine Folly: The Essential Guide to Wine* by Madeline Puckette
5. Demetria Winery, https://www.demetriaestate.com

Chapter 16

The Aroma of Aesthetic Extravagance

The Art of Fragrance

JASON MCCONNELL

Christ in the House of Simon (1440's) by Deiric Bouts the Elder

Deiric Bouts (1415–1475) was an early Netherlandish painter. He came from Haarlem, where he likely received his early training. His style was influenced by Rogier van der Weyden and Jan van Eyck. Later he settled in the university city of Louvain and was appointed city painter in 1468. He was among the first northern painters to utilize a single vanishing point.

Bouts's painting *Christ in the House of Simon* portrays a narrow, vaulted room, on the left of which is a window providing a glimpse of the landscape outside. Simon the Leper sits with his guests at a table set for a meal. To the left of the table, a woman bends down to anoint Jesus's feet with her hair. An alabaster jar of perfume is resting beside her hand. The host, the only one present wearing shoes, watches with wonder, while Peter (beside him) observes the incident with disgust and disapproval. The youthful John, at the head of the table, draws the attention of the donor, a Dominican monk. The latter kneels with hands raised in prayer and, as if he dares not look, averts his gaze.

CALL TO WORSHIP (2 CORINTHIANS 2:14–17)

Leader: But thanks be to God, who always leads us as captives in Christ's triumphal procession and uses us to spread the aroma of the knowledge of him everywhere.

People: For we are to God the pleasing aroma of Christ among those who are being saved and those who are perishing.

Leader: To the one we are an aroma that brings death; to the other, an aroma that brings life. And who is equal to such a task?

People: Unlike so many, we do not peddle the word of God for profit. On the contrary, in Christ we speak before God with sincerity, as those sent from God.

HYMN "A SINNER FORGIVEN" BY JEREMIAH J. CALLAHAN (1851)

To the hall of the feast came the sinful and fair;
She heard in the city that Jesus was there;
Unheeding the splendor that blazed on the board,
She silently knelt at the feet of the Lord,
She silently knelt at the feet of the Lord.

The frown and the murmur went round thro' them all,
That one so unhallowed should tread in that hall;
And some said the poor would be objects more meet,
As the wealth of her perfume she showered on His feet,
As the wealth of her perfume she showered on His feet.

She heard but the Savior; she spoke but with sighs;
she dared not look up to the heaven of His eyes;
And hot tears gushed forth at each heave of her breast,
As her lips to His sandals were throbbingly pressed;
As her lips to His sandals were throbbingly pressed.

In the sky, after tempest, as shineth the bow,
In glance of the sunshine, as melteth the snow,
He looked on that lost one: her sins were forgiv'n,
And the sinner went forth in the beauty of Heav'n;
And the sinner went forth in the beauty of Heav'n.

SCRIPTURE READING (MARK 14:1–11)

Now the Passover and the Festival of Unleavened Bread were only two days away, and the chief priests and the teachers of the law were scheming to arrest Jesus secretly and kill him. "But not during the festival," they said, "or the people may riot."

While he was in Bethany, reclining at the table in the home of Simon the Leper, a woman came with an alabaster jar of very expensive perfume, made of pure nard. She broke the jar and poured the perfume on his head.

Some of those present were saying indignantly to one another, "Why this waste of perfume? It could have been sold for more than a year's wages and the money given to the poor." And they rebuked her harshly.

"Leave her alone," said Jesus. "Why are you bothering her? She has done a beautiful thing to me. The poor you will always have with you, and you can help them any time you want. But you will not always have me. She did what she could. She poured perfume on my body beforehand to prepare for my burial. Truly I tell you, wherever the gospel is preached throughout the world, what she has done will also be told, in memory of her."

Then Judas Iscariot, one of the Twelve, went to the chief priests to betray Jesus to them. They were delighted to hear this and promised to give him money. So he watched for an opportunity to hand him over.

THEOLOGICAL REFLECTION

In his book *Culture Care: Reconnecting with Beauty for Our Common Lives*, renowned Japanese-American painter Mokoto Fujimura tells a powerful story about the time his wife infuriated him by bringing home a bouquet of flowers. Listen to the story in his own words:

> "As newlyweds, my wife and I began our journey with very little. After Judy and I got married in the summer of 1983, after college, we moved to Connecticut for Judy to pursue her master's degree in marriage counseling. I taught at a special education school and painted from home. We had a tight budget and often had to ration our food (lots of tuna cans!) just to get through the week.
>
> One evening I was sitting alone, waiting for Judy to come home to our small apartment, worried about how we were going to afford the rent and pay for necessities over the weekend. Our refrigerator was empty, and I had no cash left.
>
> Then Judy walked in and had brought home a bouquet of flowers. I got really upset.
>
> "How could you think of buying flowers if we can't even eat?" I remember saying, frustrated. Judy's reply has been etched in my heart for over thirty years now. "We need to feed our souls too!" The irony is that I'm an artist. I am the one, supposedly, feeding people's souls. But in worrying for tomorrow, the stoic responsibility I felt to make ends meet, to survive, I failed to be an artist. Judy was the artist: she brought home a bouquet.
>
> I do not remember what we ended up eating that day (probably tuna fish.) But I do remember that particular bouquet of flowers. I painted them. "We need to feed our souls too!
>
> Those words still resonate with me today. Is Judy still right? Do we, as human beings, need more than food and shelter? Do we need beauty in our lives? Given our limited resources, how do we cultivate and care for our souls?"[1]

For just a moment, put yourself in Mokoto Fujimura's place. How would you have reacted to Judy's exhibit of aesthetic extravagance? Would

---

1. Fujimura, *Culture Care*, 15–16.

you have complained about her choice of aesthetic impracticality over nutritional necessity? Be honest, which would you have valued more, a bouquet of flowers or a basket of bread?

This story compels us to contemplate the question: Do our souls need beauty as much as our bodies need bread? What value do you place on art and aesthetic beauty in our life?

Jesus helps us answer some of these questions in Mark 14:1–11, where we encounter the surprising scene of Jesus defending an act of aesthetic extravagance against the conventional concerns of his disciples. As we examine this story together, notice how Jesus values art, aesthetics, and beauty for our common lives. You just might become convinced that beholding beauty is essential for a healthy soul.

An Act of Aromatic Extravagance

It was a few days before the Passover Feast. As Jerusalem swelled with people from all corners of the country to celebrate the sacred Jewish holiday, the chief priests and teachers of the law were conspiring to kill Jesus.

But just three miles outside Jerusalem, in the little village of Bethany, Jesus and his disciples were attending an intimate dinner party at the home of Simon the Leper. We don't know much about Simon or the reason for this meal. He was probably one of the lepers whom Jesus healed; perhaps the meal was given as an expression of gratitude. Mark doesn't tell us what was on the menu that night, but in a kosher home like this, we can assume that neither shrimp scampi nor pulled-pork barbeque appeared on their dinner plates.

After the meal was finished and everyone was relaxing around the table, a woman came to Jesus with an alabaster jar of very expensive perfume. Mark doesn't tell us the woman's name, but John's gospel reveals that it was Mary, the sister of Martha and Lazarus, who were also from the village of Bethany. We don't know how Mary acquired this alabaster jar of pure nard, but we know that it was rare and expensive because spikenard was imported all the way from India (and back in those days, Amazon Prime didn't offer free delivery).

Nevertheless, Mary took her most precious earthly possession, broke the jar, and poured a year's worth of wages over Jesus's head, and as John's gospel tells us, she also poured some on his feet and she washed them with her hair. What an extraordinary expression of aromatic art and aesthetic extravagance! What a demonstrative display of devotion to Jesus!

Can you smell the fragrance that filled the room that evening? Are your senses aroused by the rare aroma that Jesus and his disciples experienced in that moment? Can you feel Mary's hands and hair rubbing the ointment into Jesus's feet—the feet that would be pierced for her transgressions in just a few days? Even though it's impossible to know, do you ever wonder about the unknown artist who distilled these plant oils into this sweet perfume—this perfume that anointed the body of God's Son before it was crucified and buried? Did this ancient perfumer have any idea how God would use his or her artistic expression to become the aroma of life in the midst of death—and not only for Christ, but for all who would dare to become his disciples?

When we consider Mary's audacious act, it implores us to think about how we express our love and worship for Jesus. Would we be willing to sacrifice our most valuable earthly possession for such an act of adoration to the Lord? Would we offer our precious time, talent, and treasure?

Wasteful Spending

Well, not everyone was impressed with this act of aesthetic extravagance. Mark does not name those who reacted negatively to the "waste" of perfume, but Matthew tells us that it was the disciples and John tells us that Judas Iscariot led the charge. (Matt 26:14) They protested by asking, "Why this waste of perfume? It could have been sold for more than a year's wages and the money given to the poor." Judas's indignant objection seemed pious, but he didn't really care about the poor. As the treasurer of the Twelve, he had a habit of dipping his fingers into the purse to satisfy his own selfish purposes.

It is also interesting how these disciples railed on Mary for her wastefulness when they were often the beneficiaries of her hospitality. I guess they never learned the proverb: "don't bite the hand that feeds you."

People always like to complain about other people's wasteful spending. For instance, how many of you have family members or coworkers who waste money? How many of you believe the government is guilty of wasteful spending? Accusations of wasteful spending are always due to differences in values. What you think is a waste, someone else may consider important; what you think is important; someone else may consider a waste. Our spending reveals what we really value!

What do you think? Was Mary's act of aesthetic extravagance a waste? Mary certainly didn't think so! Did Mary not care about the poor? I'm sure she did, but she valued Jesus more. What do you value most in your life?

A Beautiful Rebuke

What did Jesus think about this act of aesthetic extravagance? We would expect him to react with the same modesty and utility as the disciples, but he doesn't. He immediately comes to Mary's defense. Instead of condemning her, he commends her aromatic action as a beautiful expression of love and gratitude toward him, and she should not be berated for it.

In addition to this being an expression of sacrificial love, Jesus interpreted Mary's artistic act as a pre-anointing of his body in preparation for burial (this is somewhat like making funeral prearrangements). Typically, bodies were anointed with perfume after death, not before. Time for such an act of adoration while Jesus was with them was running out. On the contrary, opportunities for helping the poor would continue. As one commentator notes, "Mary seems to have been the only one who was sensitive to the impending death of Jesus and who was willing to give a material expression of her esteem for him. Jesus's reply shows his appreciation of her act of devotion."

In fact, Jesus was so moved by Mary's gesture that he says, "Truly I tell you, wherever the gospel is preached throughout the world, what she has done will also be told, in memory of her." In a stroke of unintentional irony, Mark quotes Jesus's prediction that this story will always be told in memory of a woman whose very name escapes him. Nonetheless, here we are some two thousand years later still retelling this story.

Even so, you may be wondering: Does Jesus's rebuke show a lack of concern for the poor? Absolutely not! Jesus constantly showed compassion for "the least of these" throughout his ministry, but he would not take this expression of love away from Mary.

Some Christians have posed questions like, "How can we feast while so many other people in the world go hungry? How can we celebrate when there is so much sadness and suffering all around us? How do we justify our lavish Thanksgiving dinners and Christmas gifts when so many people live in poverty? How can we ever purchase a painting, attend a concert, go to a play, buy a bottle of perfume, or bring home a bouquet of flowers when there are so many more practical needs in life? Is there ever a place for aesthetic extravagance in the Christian life?

Here is how I believe Jesus would answer these questions: balance! If we constantly neglect the poor to support an extravagant lifestyle, we are guilty of selfishness. On the other hand, occasional extravagance can be a beautiful expression of love, and it could have a profound and lasting impact on our souls. So, enjoy your holiday feasts and celebrations; just don't do it every day! And when it comes to art, aesthetics, and beauty, we must remember the importance of feeding our souls!

A Costly Betrayal

Immediately, after the anointing, we learn about Judas's duplicity as he offers to betray Jesus to the chief priests. Mary's extravagant deed of devotion stands in stark contrast to Judas's act of betrayal. Isn't it ironic that right after Judas complains about Mary's extravagant waste, we find him betraying Jesus to the chief priests for a few silver coins? He is willing to sacrifice Jesus to obtain material gain for himself; on the other hand, Mary sacrificed her most precious material possession for Jesus. Mary will always be remembered for her act of devotion; Judas will always be remembered for his act of betrayal.

These verses cause us to ask some penetrating questions: How will I be remembered when I'm gone? Will I be remembered for my greed or my generosity? Will I be remembered for my duplicity or my devotion? Will I be remembered for my selfishness or my sacrifice? Will I be remembered for my betrayal or my faithfulness to Jesus?

Conclusion

My grandmother has always loved perfume. I remember when I was a child, every time I went into a department store with her, she would stop by the perfume counter and dab her wrists from one of the tester bottles. Then we would smell the aroma together. My family wasn't particularly poor, but my grandfather refused to buy perfume for my grandmother. As a hard-working blue-collar pragmatist, he considered perfume an unnecessary extravagance.

When I was about twelve years old, my sister and I wanted to buy our grandmother a bottle of perfume for Christmas. But we didn't want to get her some cheap drug store perfume; we wanted to get her favorite fragrance, "White Diamonds" by Elizabeth Taylor. So, a few weeks before Christmas, we scraped all of our money together and slipped away to the department store perfume counter.

When we asked the clerk how much for a bottle of White Diamonds, she replied, "Fifty dollars." Our eyes almost popped out of our heads! I was tempted to ask her if there were real diamonds in the bottle, but instead, I just asked if she had a smaller bottle. She said, "I'm sorry but this is our smallest bottle." Our hopes were dashed when we only counted forty-two dollars. But after the clerk heard our story and saw my sister sobbing, she took pity on us and paid the remaining balance herself. To our adolescent minds, it appeared to be a Christmas miracle.

When Christmas morning came, we were just as excited for Grandma to open her gift as we were to open our own gifts. As she ripped off the wrapping paper, a look of astonishment came over her and tears of gratitude flooded down her face. I will never forget that moment and I'll never forget the aroma of White Diamonds! That Christmas day, not only did I learn something about the cost of perfume, but I learned something about the aroma of aesthetic extravagance.

It's no wonder Jesus said that Mary's act would always be remembered! Even long after Jesus ascended back to his Father in heaven, I don't think the disciples ever forgot that fragrance of pure spikenard that filled Simon's house that night! Perhaps they even remembered this amazing aroma when they began their own journey through the valley of the shadow of death. Sometimes our souls need to be fed by an act of aesthetic extravagance!

PRAYER

Dear Lord, help us realize that our souls need beauty as much as our bodies need bread. As Mary's extravagant expression of love has been remembered throughout the generations, help us remember that everything we have is a gift from you! May we use our most precious possessions to worship and glorify you!

Protect us from the pragmatism and duplicity of Jesus's disciples. May we always be sensitive to the plight of the poor, but may we also be willing to worship you with uninhibited extravagance. Wherever we go, use us to spread the fragrance of Christ; may we be the aroma of Christ to those who are being saved and to those who are perishing! Amen.

DISCUSSION QUESTIONS

1. What are some of your favorite fragrances, natural and created? How do these fragrances affect your body, mind, and soul?
2. Has a fragrance ever transported you to another place in time? Why does the sense of smell (along with our other senses) have the ability to bring back memories?
3. Why do so many Christians (and people in general) value utilitarian frugality over aesthetic extravagance?

4. Has anyone ever given you a gift of aesthetic extravagance? For example, a costly fragrance, expensive jewelry, a luxurious painting, an elegant meal, a rare bottle of wine? How did you respond to the gift and gift-giver?

SPIRITUAL EXERCISES

1. Go for a walk in one of your favorite outdoor locations. Smell the various fragrances (e.g. pine trees in the forest, the salt spray of the ocean, a field of wildflowers). Praise God for creating such a vast array of beautiful aromas!
2. Go to a perfume counter at a department store. Sample some fragrances and appreciate the perfumer's craft!
3. Watch a film about perfume! *Perfume: The Story of a Murderer*, *The Scent of a Woman*, or *Coco Chanel and Igor Stravinsky*. Ponder the aesthetic power of perfume!
4. Read a book or watch an instructional video about how to create perfumes. Then attempt to invent your own fragrance.
5. Burn incense during a worship service, even if this is not your liturgical tradition. Explain this tradition from a biblical, historical, and aesthetic perspective.
6. Host a foot-washing service at the church on an evening during Holy Week (perhaps Maundy Thursday or Good Friday). Instead of a traditional foot-washing ceremony that focuses on Jesus washing his disciples' feet (John 13), read Mark 14:1–11 and quietly meditate on Mary's extravagant act of pouring perfume over Jesus's head and washing his feet with her hair. Spike a basin of water with a fragrant perfume and smell the fragrance of humility while the participants wash each other's feet. Sing Jeremiah J. Callahan's beautiful hymn "A Sinner Forgiven" together.

RESOURCES FOR FURTHER REFLECTION

1. *The Community of the Beautiful: A Theological Aesthetics* by Alejandro R. Garcia-Rivera

2. *A Redemptive Theology of Art: Restoring Godly Aesthetics to Doctrine and Culture* by David A. Covington

3. *Essence and Alchemy: A Natural History of Perfume* by Mandy Aftel

4. *Cult Perfumes: The World's Most Exclusive Perfumeries* by Tessa Williams

5. *Homemade Perfume: Create Exquisite, Naturally Scented Products to Fill Your Life with Botanical Aromas* by Anya McCoy

6. *Perfume: Joy, Scandal, Sin—A Cultural History of Fragrance from 1750 to the Present* by Richard Stamelman

Reclaiming the Arts Through Worship

Kenneth J. Barnes

When the magnificent cave paintings of Altamira in Santander, Spain were first discovered in the late nineteenth century, prehistorians of the day dismissed their ancient origins, assuming they were the work of local contemporary artists. They simply rejected the notion that our cro-magnon ancestors could have possessed the skills necessary to produce such life-like works of art, on such a grand scale, and with such technical precision. Soon however, other caves of a similar nature began to appear in the Dordogne region of France, where the presence of paleolithic deposits blocking their entrances ruled out the possibility of a modern provenance. Carbon dating has indeed confirmed these sites to be prehistoric, dating back tens of thousands of years, but the question remains: What were these drawings for? Were they science or were they art, or were they something else altogether?

Some years later, an even more remarkable discovery was made near the Franco-Spanish border at a place called L'Aven that may help to answer those questions. There in a nearly inaccessible cave, three brothers crawled on their hands and knees to discover what can best be described as some kind of primitive "sanctuary," with what appeared to be an "altar" of sorts, complete with various "votive" objects (bones, tools, and other artifacts), placed below a prominent drawing, not of an animal, but a mythical "deity" figure, suggesting that these prehistoric sites may in fact have served a religious purpose. Perhaps in their desire to better understand their physical environment, they employed the mimetic nature of art; but perhaps, in their desire to better understand the very nature of their existence, their art became their worship?

This hypothesis would fit well with the theory posited by Oxford University material scientist Professor Andrew Briggs and Oxford-based artist Roger Wagner in their exceptional tome entitled *The Penultimate Curiosity*, where they argue that all scientific inquiry "swims in the slipstream" of the "ultimate curiosity," which is the answer to the great question: "Why?"[1] This is a question that is sometimes expressed in words and ideas, but can sometimes be better expressed in "unutterable" ways—in music, in sculpture, in painting, in art!

Why art? Because, as Dr. Horn suggests at the beginning of this book, at its core, art is about beauty seeking transcendence, and the ultimate source of transcendence can only be found in what twentieth-century theologian Paul Tillich called our very "ground of being," the "God above God"[2] whose essence is truly indescribable. Indescribable perhaps, but not "unknowable"; revelation gives us a glimpse of the divine essence, but as the apostle Paul admits: "For now we see only a reflection as in a mirror; then we shall see face to face. Now I know in part; then I shall know fully, even as I am fully known" (1 Cor 13:12). And so, we are left to dwell in our "already but not yet" existence, a no-man's land between imminence and transcendence, ill-equipped to express our deepest desire to reconnect with the God from whom we are estranged yet compelled to do so with whatever tools we have at our disposal: the scriptures, our liturgies, our songs of praise, even our Holy Spirit-induced "unutterable groans" of prayer (Rom 8:26), and more.

But what does all of this have to do with our study? What does this have to do with the question of how we can "reclaim the arts through worship"? I would propose that we don't need to "reclaim" anything. I say, instead, that we need only to release ourselves from the shackles of our own traditions and allow ourselves the freedom to "worship God in Spirit and in truth" (John 4:25). Surely, not all art is worship, but if done properly and in alignment with the nature and character of the God in whose image we are created, the God of Scripture, who is the artist *par excellence*, all worship, I contend, may properly be called "art"!

I believe this to be at the very heart of Dr. Jason McConnell's argument in chapter 1, where he frames both art and worship within the pericope of the creation narratives. God in his majesty and wisdom has brought forth

---

1. Wagner and Briggs, *Penultimate Curiosity*, 53.
2. Tillich, *Courage to Be*, 186.

order from chaos and beauty from nothingness, inviting his creatures to become co-creators, bestowing upon us the pallet of the natural world and the agency of body, mind, and spirit.

Similarly, in chapters 2 through 4, reverends McCarley, Cahan, and Roberts stir our imaginations with visions of God the painter, God the sculptor, even God the haberdasher! But God is all of those things, and we should feel free to follow his lead in our most sacred acts of worship. Beautiful images need not lead to idolatry. On the contrary, they should take us beyond the mere images themselves, to the source of beauty itself. They should point us toward God. While the works of art that adorn the halls of the Louvre, the Met, and countless other museums often depict religious scenes, they pale in comparison to similar works that grace the walls of countless churches, cathedrals and chapels. Why? Because they are fulfilling their *telos*, by inviting worshipers to look past the brilliant use of light, to the very source of light; to look past the deft hand of the artist to his longing soul.

This is made clear by the experience of worshipers who enter the chapel at New College, Oxford. Surrounded by the classic works of El Greco, Giordano and others, one's eyes and soul are first gripped by a modern sculpture, the stark and haunting figure of Lazarus by Sir Jacob Epstein (1948), that stands in the antechapel, where all who enter must pass. The image of a man, freed from the grave, in a pose that evokes an existence somewhere between life and death, the fellows returning to college having experienced the horrors of World War II, no doubt saw in that statue a glimpse of their own reality. Where were they? Why were they alive, when so many of their brothers in arms were left behind? What is the meaning of life? Is death the end for us all? Or is there something beyond the grave? Is there redemption? Is there resurrection? Is the one who raised Lazarus, truly "the resurrection and the life" (John 11:25)? All thoughts beyond words—all come to life in one simple work of art.

And yes, even the clothes we wear can be integral to our worship. God chose not to adorn his image-bearers with the plumage and colorful array of other species, leaving it to us to clothe ourselves in splendor, but not without example or direction. From God's own act of kindness toward Adam and Eve in the garden (Gen 3:21), to the detailed instructions of Exodus 28, God cares deeply about our adornment, especially as it relates to our worship. Using clothes to set apart the priests of old, their garments became indelibly linked to their office, so much so, that when King Saul ordered their massacre, the Bible refers to them as "eighty-five persons who wore the linen ephod" (1 Sam 22:18). They weren't merely recognized by their garb, they were defined by it. Perhaps in our desire to make worship less extravagant and more "accessible," we've inadvertently lost the power of fashion to solemnize our services?

In chapters 5 and 6, reverends Romig and Weiler remind us of the place of dance in our worship, a practice attested to throughout the Bible, performed by those whose words fail them as they rejoice in the power, majesty, and grace of God. Who wouldn't want to "dance as David danced" (2 Sam 6:14) with "all his might" as he celebrated the return of the Ark of the Covenant? In fact, we are implored to dance by the psalmist, and to sing to the glory of God (see Chapters Nine and Ten by Revs. Smith and Bogertman):

> Hallelujah!
> Praise God in His sanctuary.
> Praise Him in His mighty heavens.
> Praise Him for His mighty acts;
> praise Him for His excellent greatness.
> Praise Him with the sound of the horn;
> praise Him with the harp and lyre.
> Praise Him with tambourine and dancing;
> praise Him with strings and flute.
> Praise Him with clashing cymbals;
> praise Him with resounding cymbals.
> Let everything that has breath praise the LORD!
> Hallelujah! (Ps.150:1–6)

Oh, how our Puritan heritage and Victorian sensibilities can obscure our deepest desires to worship God with abandon! There is a place for decorum and order in worship, but that doesn't preclude the proper use of music and dance, even in the most traditional settings. Several years ago, in the chapel of the seminary where I teach, the usual "Presbyterian-style" worship service went *off-piste* and allowed a modern dance troupe to perform a piece celebrating the resurrection of Jesus. Dressed in all white, the young performers and worshippers moved gracefully across the sanctuary, expressing the inexpressible truth of life overcoming death.

Among the dancers, however, was a figure known to everyone in the chapel; a sixty-five-year-old seminary professor, dressed in tights and tanktop moved with grace and poise that defied his years, that brought awe and wonder to the congregation. Seemingly out of place, he "danced as David danced," with joy, with gusto, in spirit and in truth. It was a seminal moment for the chapel, and one that confirmed for me the place of music and dance in worship.

What then, is the place of theatre in worship? Can even "secular" plays, convey the message of the Gospel, in subtle, yet highly effective ways that we may rightly call "worship"? After all, the Apostle Paul tells us that we are to "offer [our] bodies as living sacrifice(s), holy and pleasing to God—this is our true and proper worship" (Rom 12:1), affirming that "in whatever [we] do, whether in word or deed" (we are to) "do it all in the name of the Lord Jesus" (Col 3:17). Surely this applies to people in the performing professions who are disciples of Christ? Jeff Miller deftly addresses these questions in Chapter Seven. I remember well however, the first time I saw the broadway musical *Les Miserables,* based on Victor Hugo's similarly entitled book. Despite his own animosity toward the Roman See, his Christian values were so deeply engrained in his soul that he produced a story of redemption that can only be described as "the gospel in disguise." In Chapter Thirteen, Rev. Bresnahan shares a similar story in his examination of Cinema as an instrument of God's grace, as he unpacks the sublime story of "Babette's Feast."

Then of course, there is the power of the written word, and its place in our worship. How easy it is for us to forget the diversity of God's own word in Scripture. The narratives of the Pentateuch are similar, yet distinct from the historic re-telling of Israel's past. The wisdom literature with its unique blend of poetry and prose, are likewise set apart from the cautionary utterances of the Prophets. The Gospels and the Book of Acts are more the "memoirs of the Apostles"[3] than strictly "biographies" and the Epistles (including the Book of Revelation) are themselves distinct from the rest of Scripture. Written by dozens of authors, in multiple languages, over hundreds, if not thousands of years, they all contribute to the rich telling of the meta-narrative of Creation, Fall, Redemption and Restitution or Consummation. They form the ultimate codex of sacred literature, but they are not the only sources at our disposal.

In Chapters Eleven and Twelve, Revs. Harrington and Coons, explore how novels, and short stories alike, with their own meta-narratives, can capture the essence of the biblical epic, and even reflect its difficult truths, its stark realities, its moments of despair and most importantly, its hope of benevolent triumph. In Chapter Eight, Rev. Daphnis, delves deeply into the power of poetry to express the lament of those whose persecution is unrelenting as he cries out "How Long Lord?" in a contemporary verse, as raw and evocative as Psalm 13 itself.

And in Chapters Fourteen and Fifteen, Rev. Roberts and Canon Bethke, set the table for us, as they explore the role of food and drink in the context of our worship. These are chapters that may surprise some people

---

3. Justin Martyr, "1 Apology," 67.

who think of food and drink as merely part of the church's *koinonia* ("fellowship"), but they are much more important than that. As I often tell my students, all profanity is vulgar, but not all vulgarity is profane. Vulgarity deals with "common" things, whether in language or actions. Profanity, however, is when something that is sacred is rendered common—that is profanity.

Hence, the taking of the Lord's name in vain, is profane, because it is meant to be holy, while having a "potty-mouth" is merely vulgar. The qualitative difference is in the intended sacredness of the object. Conversely however, in the sacraments, God does the exact opposite. In the sacraments, God takes common things and makes them holy. In baptism, the most common "element" of all—water—is made holy, because God is using it to sanctify the life of a believer. The same is true of the Lord's Table, or Holy Communion, where the common elements of bread and wine are made holy, because they become for us the body and blood of our Lord and Saviour Jesus Christ. The qualitative difference here is how those common elements are being used to glorify God. Following that pattern, isn't it possible that we could use food and drink in any number of "worshipful" ways? In a country where thirty-seven million people are "food insecure,"[4] the possibilities seem endless.

Lastly, we have Chapter Sixteen, a bookend to Chapter One by Dr. McConnell, who challenges us to re-think the notion of "aesthetic extravagance." In our culture we often confuse extravagance with "hedonism" but the two are not necessarily congruent. Yes, there are times when people go "over the top," when they are wasteful and self-indulgent, and the church is not immune to this behavior. There are times, however, when we need to express in material ways the very same emotions as the aforementioned singers and dancers, painters and sculptors, writers, and aesthetes. There are times when we need to give thanks to the Lord who came "that [we] may have life and have it abundantly" (John 10:10), and that may include "aesthetic extravagance" in any number of forms. We cannot ever sufficiently thank God for all God has done for us, but neither can we over-express our gratitude, as insufficient and petty as it may actually be.

In some ways, this volume is an attempt by its authors to express our gratitude to God, for the gifts of worship and art. It is our modest offering to those who wish to explore the possibility of bringing them more closely together, in new and faithful ways, to the glory of God and the building of God's Kingdom. Amen.

---

4. "Shadow of Hunger," *New York Times*, https://www.nytimes.com/interactive/2020/09/02/magazine/food-insecurity-hunger-us.html.

Bibliography

Abrams, Meyer H. *The Mirror and the Lamp: Romantic Theory and the Critical Tradition*. Oxford: Oxford University Press, 1953.
Ackerman, Susan. "Dance." In *Eerdmans Dictionary of the Bible*, edited by David Noel Freedman, 311. Grand Rapids: Eerdmans, 2000.
Austen, Jane. *Pride and Prejudice*. New York: Random House, 1992.
Britannica "How a Rejected Block of Marble Became the World's Most Famous Statue" https://www.britannica.com/story/how-a-rejected-block-of-marble-became-the-worlds-most-famous-statue.
Bruner, Dale. *Matthew: The Churchbook Volume 2*. Grand Rapids: Eerdmans, 2004.
Butterworth, Neil. *Haydn, His Life and Times*. Kent: Midas Books, 1977.
Calvin, John. *Institutes of the Christian Religion*. Peabody, Mass: Hendrickson, 2008.
———. *Letters of John Calvin*, vol. 2, edited by Jules Bonnet. Philadelphia, PA: Presbyterian Board of Publication, 1858.
Dickens, Charles. *A Tale of Two Cities*. Bradford, UK: Watermill, 1983.
Dinesen, Isak. *Anecdotes of Destiny and Ehrengard*. New York: Vintage, 1993.
Dostoyevsky, Fyodor. *Crime and Punishment*. Mineola, NY: Dover, 2002.
Franklin Foer. "Attention is the Beginning of Devotion." *The Atlantic*, May 19, 2019. https://www.theatlantic.com/technology/archive/2019/05/mary-olivers-poetry-captures-our-relationship-technology/589039/.
Garber, Steve. "Singing Songs that the Whole World Can Hear." *The Washington Institute for Faith, Vocation and Culture*. https://washingtoninst.org/singing-songs-that-the-whole-world-can-hear/.
Lewis, C. S. *The Weight of Glory: And Other Addresses*. Grand Rapids: Eerdmans, 1965.
———. *The Last Battle*. New York: HarperCollins, 1994.
Johnson, James Weldon. *The Book of American Negro Poetry*, Monee, IL: Grindl, 2015.
Justin Martyr. "1 Apology." In *Ante-Nicene Fathers*, edited by Alexander Roberts, James Donaldson, and A. Cleveland Coxe, translated by Marcus Dods and George Reith. Buffalo, NY: Christian Literature, 1885.
Kreglinger, Gisela. *The Spirituality of Wine*. Grand Rapids: Eerdmans, 2016.
McGrath, Alister. *Theology: The Basics*. Hoboken, NJ: Blackwell, 2018.
McKelvey, Douglas Kaine. *Every Moment Holy*. Nashville: Rabbit Room, 2017.
O'Connor, Flannery. *The Complete Stories*. New York: Farrar, Straus and Giroux, 1971.
Oliver, Mary. *Upstream: Selected Essays*. New York: Penguin, 2016.

Percy, Walker. *Signposts in a Strange Land: Essays*. New York: Open Road Media, 2011.
Peterson, Eugene. *Tell it Slant*. Grand Rapids: Eerdmans, 2008.
Piper, John. "You Live in a God-Entranced World." *Crossway*.
Schmemann, Alexander. *For the Life of the World*. Yonkers, NY: Saint Vladimir's Seminary Press, 2018.
Schönberg, Claude-Michel. "Les Misérables : a Musical." Act I. Milwaukee, WI :Alain Boublil Music, 1998.
Seat, Leroy. "The Bible and the Newspaper." Word and Way, May 5, 2020. https://wordandway.org/2020/05/05/the-bible-and-the-newspaper/.
Smith, James K. A. *You Are What You Love: The Spiritual Power of Habit*. Grand Rapids: Brazos, 2016.
Solzhenitsyn, Aleksandr. "Art—for Man's Sake." *The New York Times*, September 30, 1972.
Sweet, Leonard. *From Tablet to Table: Where Community is Found and Identity is Formed*. Colorado Springs, CO: NavPress, 2014.
Thomas, Gary. *Cherish: The One Word that Changes Everything for Your Marriage*. Grand Rapids: Zondervan, 2017.
Tillich, Paul. *The Courage to Be*. New Haven: Yale University Press. 1952.
Tolkien, J.R.R. *The Hobbit*. New York: Ballantine, 1982.
Turner, Steve. *Imagine: A Vision For Christians in the Arts*. Downers Grove, IL: InterVarsity Press, 2001.
Wagner, Roger, and Andrew Briggs. *The Penultimate Curiosity*. Oxford: Oxford University Press. 2019.
Walton, John. *Genesis*. NIV Application Commentary, edited by Terry Muck. Grand Rapids: Zondervan, 2001.
Wilder, Thornton. *Our Town*. New York: HarperPerennial, 2003.
Wirzba, Norman. *Food and Faith: A Theology of Eating*. 2nd edition. Cambridge: Cambridge University Press, 2019.
Wright, N. T. *Ask N. T. Wright Anything Podcast*. Premiere Christian Radio.

www.ingramcontent.com/pod-product-compliance
Lightning Source LLC
Chambersburg PA
CBHW060607230426
43670CB00011B/2004